Student Life: A Survival Guide

Natasha Roe

Student Helpbook Series

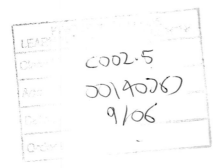

C002.5
0019076)
9/06

Student Life: A Survival Guide – fourth edition

Published by Lifetime Careers Publishing, 7 Ascot Court, White Horse Business Park, Trowbridge BA14 0XA

© Lifetime Careers Wiltshire Ltd, 2006

ISBN 1 904979 01 7

ISBN-13 978 190497901 2

Printed and bound by Cromwell Press Ltd, Trowbridge
Cover design by Lesley May
Illustrations by Joe Wright

Contents

About the author

Natasha Roe is an experienced advice and education writer who spent ten years producing publications and websites to support national and regional television programmes. She has written for adults, young people and children on topics as diverse as disability, social history, education, health, the arts and work. She is a former sabbatical editor of the University of London newspaper *London Student* and has been a student adviser on helplines run by Capital Radio.

She now runs Red Pencil Projects providing writing and editorial services to a variety of media, commercial and not-for-profit organisations.

Acknowledgements

Anecdotes were researched and compiled by Isabelle Brewerton, while she was a fourth-year modern and medieval languages student, Corpus Christi College, Cambridge University.

With thanks to the following students and graduates who have contributed their experience and advice:

Phil Agulnik, Claire Baldwin, Paul Blundell, Isabelle Brewerton, Andy Bridges, Sarah Brown, Cherry Canovan, Jeremy Carlton, Sukanta Chowdhury, Jonathan Clayton, Mona Lisa Cook, Susanna Craig, Elizabeth Hardaker, Jennifer Hogan, Katie Hogan, Deborah Hyde, Allan Jones, Rhian Jones, Natalie King, Katherine Lawrey, Alastair Lee, Tony Leighton, Rob Lucas, Phil Marsh, Rhiannon Michael, Phil Mitchell, Andrew Newsome, Amy North, Samantha Northey, Phil Pearce, Martin Petchey, Anna Roberts, Peter Rodger, Vicky Spencer, Andrew Stephenson, Amanda Warburton, Lindsey Wilson, William Wilson, Katrina Woods.

With additional thanks to Alec Leggat for his support and to Tam and Edie.

Please note: You'll find that the term 'university' has been used throughout this book as shorthand for 'university or college/institute of higher education'.

You've made it

Congratulations! Whether you've known you've had a place at university for several months or you've only just found out that your clearing place has come through – you *are* going to university.

Once the elation has died down you are going to need to get practical. Going to university is a big step in most people's lives and there are lots of things that you need to get organised before you go. You are also going to have to get your head round the fact that you may be leaving home, moving away from family and friends, and living on your own for the first time. You will certainly be meeting new people and studying in a completely different way. And these days, going to university costs so you are going to have to learn to manage on a tight budget. One or two of these changes are a lot to take on – but all of them at once? No wonder going to university can appear quite daunting.

'It was a bit of a culture shock starting university. On the first day when your parents leave you in your room, with all your stuff just dumped there, it takes a while to sink in. But then you meet other people and talk to them, which takes your mind off things. And the comforting thing is that everybody else is in the same situation.'

**Phil Pearce, fifth-year business studies student,
Luton University**

However, if you know what you need to do and when you need to do it then change is much easier to manage. *Student Life: A Survival Guide* can help lead you through each step. Starting from what to do before you go and when you first arrive, through to what will be expected of you during your course. Along the way we have tips on how to make the pennies stretch and how to survive living away from home while staying safe and healthy. We'll even look at how you can make the most of your time at university and the choices you face at the end. So if you ever feel unsure about what to do and when to do it, *Student Life* can lend a hand.

Chapter one
Before you go

This chapter covers:

- Applying for student loans
- Deciding where to live
- Extra arrangements
- Travelling there
- Packing
- Insurance
- Sorting out money
- Life skills
- Saying goodbye
- Your expectations

Although it is really tempting to just kick back and enjoy the summer before you start university, there are some things that you need to have done before you set off on your merry way. Unfortunately, they are very important things, and if you don't meet the deadlines you might end up having to pay all your own living costs and tuition fees or not having a roof over your head. Stay on top of the game by following our guide.

Applying for student loans

You will be aware that, from 2006 entry, the arrangements for student finances are changing significantly in England. The maximum amount students will be asked to contribute to their tuition fees will rise to £3000, but a new student loan will be available to cover this contribution. The student loan to cover living expenses will also increase to more than the rate of inflation. You will have to start paying back both student loans once you are earning more than

£15,000. There will also be a new maintenance grant for students from low-income families.

There is more information on student loans and tuition fees, including how the rules differ in different parts of the country, in Chapter four. Make sure you read up so that you are clear about what you are applying for.

You will need to apply for financial support (loans and grants) once you have applied for a place on a university course. *Don't wait until you have a firm offer.* Application forms (online and paper-based) are usually available from March onwards.

You need to contact the assessment authority for the area you are living in when you apply to go to university *not* the area where you are going to be studying. Students living in England and Wales before they start their course need to contact their **Local Education Authority** (contact details available at www.dfes.gov.uk/studentsupport). Students living in Northern Ireland need to contact their local **Education and Library Board** (contact details available from www. deni.gov.uk), while students living in Scotland should contact the **Student Awards Agency for Scotland** (on 0845 111 1711 or www. student-support-saas.gov.uk).

The assessment agency will look at your circumstances and those of your family (parents, spouse, partner) and work out what you are entitled to.

To apply for student loan(s), you will need to provide:

- National Insurance number (contact the Inland Revenue National Insurance helpline on 0845 915 7006 if you can't find this)

- birth certificate or a valid passport

- evidence of your family income

- any other supporting documents your assessment authority may ask for.

Make sure you complete your application fully and return it by the deadline. The deadlines change each year and are published by the relevant assessment authorities.

Deciding where to live

Most students choose to live in university accommodation, certainly for the first year, providing they get the option. Accommodation isn't sorted out automatically – you need to apply for a place. Usually, you will be sent a brochure outlining the options once you have accepted a confirmed offer at a university. If you don't get this, ring the university and ask them for details. The range and availability of accommodation varies dramatically around the country, so find out as much as possible about what is available.

'After I got my A level results I got a booklet with information about the different halls of residence available but to be honest I didn't actually visit any of them. I chose my hall based on the facilities available. Mine has a lot of stuff organised for the students – music, drama and sports. You socialise a lot there and it was a great way of meeting people.'

Susanna Craig, first-year politics and parliamentary studies student, Leeds University

---

You are likely to be offered a choice of halls of residence and shared self-catering flats and houses. Increasingly, halls, flats and houses may be built in student 'villages' with shared communal spaces and facilities, such as launderettes, sports halls and bars. Most universities also have houses that they rent in the area and then sublet to students, although these may not be available to first-years. You are likely to have a wider choice of university accommodation if you study at a campus university. If your university has limited accommodation or you are offered a place through clearing, then you may have to make your own independent living arrangements. Read more about the types of housing available to students in Chapter six.

Bear in mind that you will be living at university for the best part of a year so take time to consider your options. Thinking about what sort of person you are may help you to decide.

Students' unions and accommodation offices have details about university accommodation and private sector housing available in the area. Many have lists of recommended landlords, landladies, housing associations and agencies.

Type of accommodation	Type of person					
	Confident about leaving home	Independent	Wants to meet students	Finds it difficult to mix	Unsure about leaving home	Wants to mix with non-students
Halls (catered)	*		*	*	*	
Halls (self-catered)	*	*	*	*		
Student house/flat	*	*	*			
Student villages	*	*	*			
Private accommodation in student areas	*	*	*			
Private accommodation in non-student areas	*	*				*
Lodger with family				*	*	
Bedsit	*	*				*
Parental home				*	*	*

Contact the accommodation office immediately if you have specific housing needs like a disability or dependants, or if you're offered a place through clearing. A place at a university that has no accommodation left, may not be for you after all. If you want to live in university accommodation, return your accommodation form with your first, second and third choices clearly marked. You may also be asked to complete a questionnaire that asks you things like your interests, if you practise a religion, whether you are vegetarian and whether you smoke. Universities try wherever possible to place students with similar lifestyles in shared accommodation, but they aren't always able to do this. However, you stand a better chance of being given your first choice of housing if you return your application form in plenty of time.

'You can't choose who you share with and they often have different interests, priorities and even morals about certain situations!'

Katie Hogan, first-year sociology student, Essex University

If you encounter problems or find that you have nowhere to live there's advice and information in Chapter six.

Should I live at home?

More students are choosing to live with their parents and save money while they study. It also saves on having to pack and you're likely to be living in nicer surroundings than students in digs. However, you may find it more difficult to meet new people and join in with university life if you aren't living on campus or with other students. Make sure you join some clubs and societies (see Chapter two) and find out from people on your course what their evening plans are. You'll also benefit from negotiating some new ground rules with your parents that acknowledge that you're an adult university student while still treating their house with respect. Get these straight before you start your course.

Extra arrangements

Some students will need to make additional arrangements with the university to make sure everything is in place to meet their needs.

Disabled students

Once you have confirmed your place, get in touch with the access or disability officer at your university. Go through all your requirements in detail and make sure that they will be able to provide everything in time. If necessary, make an appointment to visit the university before term starts to run through the arrangements. Many universities will be able to offer information and advice about the types of support and the additional funding available for disabled students (see also *Disabled students*, page 78).

Get in touch with **SKILL: the National Bureau for Students with Disabilities**. It provides advice on all aspects of student life including funding, welfare, work experience, jobs and equipment and produces over 30 publications. There's lots of information on their website at www.skill.org.uk Alternatively, you can ring the information line on 0800 328 5050 on Tuesday and Thursday afternoons or dial textphone on 0800 068 2422. There are also SKILL offices covering Wales, Northern Ireland and Scotland; contact details are on the website.

You may also find *The Disabled Students' Guide to University 2005* helpful. It is published by Trotman, priced £21.99.

Mature students

If you are a mature student (over 21) you may have lived away from home before and be confident about being able to fend for yourself. However, you may want to live and mix with other students of your age. Contact the university and find out what provisions they make for mature students, some have special introductory sessions and societies.

Trotman has published *The Mature Students' Guide to Higher Education* priced £19.99, which is available from www.trotman.co.uk

Students with children

If you have children then you will need to sort out nursery and crèche places before term starts. If you are eligible, you also need to apply for a Childcare and Dependants Grant (see *Students with dependants*, page 79). Larger universities may have additional grants available to students with children and even child support officers who can offer advice. Contact your university to find out what it offers.

International students

If you are planning to study in the UK first you have to make sure that you meet the eligibility criteria. Then you need to find out about the fees you might be liable for. International students are liable for the full cost of their tuition fees, unless they apply successfully for scholarships and bursaries. You can find information on courses and fees, scholarships and bursaries, plus advice on studying and living in the UK from www.educationuk.org or www.ukcosa.org.uk

The British Council also produces a publication *Studying and Living in the UK,* which you can download from www.britishcouncil.org/education/qdu/info.htm#students

Once you arrive at university you will probably find that the international students' officer has arranged additional orientation and social activities during freshers' week (see Chapter two).

If you are a student from a European Union country, then the financial support is broadly the same as for students from the UK. You just need to be careful that you meet the application deadlines. More information is available from the DfES website at www.dfes. gov.uk/studentsupport/eustudents/index.shtml

Travelling there

Decide how you are going to get to university for the start of term. It's worth planning this in advance as it will affect what you pack, how you pack it and whether you need to have some things sent on to you.

If you can, persuading a parent or friend to give you a lift to university is definitely the best option. Don't worry about losing 'street cred' by having your parents drop you off as most people will be in the same position. If you have to travel to university on public transport then be careful about what you take and how you pack it (see *Packing,* page 14). Contact the bus, train or coach company a month before you have to travel. Interrogate them thoroughly about the cheapest way you can get there. Most will have Apex and Super Apex fares, which are much cheaper than buying tickets on the day. Also ask about the luggage arrangements or limitations. For instance, you can't take bikes on some train routes and there's often a luggage limit on coaches. You may need to arrange to have your belongings delivered to university by a courier company – try www.locateacourier.net for details.

If you have a lot of things to carry then plan your journey very carefully and allow plenty of time, particularly if it involves changes. What is normally a leisurely five-minute stroll across a platform can be quite a different matter when you are laden down like a pack mule, so avoid short connection times. Also remember that you have to get from the station to the university. Don't leave yourself stranded in a strange area. Phone the university beforehand and get details about how to get there from the station, including the cost of a taxi.

Packing

'I decided what I was going to take to university in a last-minute, really stressed frenzy and would not recommend that approach to anyone else! The only thing I know I did right was asking what kitchen stuff I really needed. Some halls are fully supplied with all kitchen stuff and others you need to take your own things.'

Elizabeth Hardaker, fourth-year biology masters student, University of Bath

Documents

When you get to university you will have 101 things to sign up for and enrol in. Many of them will ask you for the same documents, some will ask you for money and lots will require a passport photo to put on various cards and files. It will be much less stressful if you are not scrabbling around to find what you need. Put all essential documents in one bag.

These should include:

- course acceptance letter, correspondence from your department, reading lists, etc
- accommodation office letter
- campus map
- documents from your local education authority and the student loan company
- travel tickets and student travel discount cards
- your National Insurance number and any tax forms you have
- your passport, birth certificate and driving licence
- your NHS medical card
- several passport-sized photographs
- insurance documents

- any medical certificates you have been asked to bring and/or your doctor's and dentist's details

- your bank details

- diary or organiser

- notebook and pen

- your wallet or purse with bank cards and cash.

The rest of what you decide to take with you will then depend largely on where you'll be living. If you're moving to a hall of residence you need far fewer domestic items than if you're renting a bedsit. If you're living in rented or self-catering accommodation then compare what is already provided with what is suggested in the checklists. You don't want to end up hardly able to open your door because you have tried to move the contents of your parents' house into your room. On the other hand, you don't want to have to return home after a couple of days because you have forgotten to pack a pair of shoes. Don't do all your packing the night before you leave. Start at least two days beforehand so you have plenty of time to think about what to take.

Wherever you live you will need:

- a kettle and some mugs with a jar of coffee and a carton of longlife milk to get you started

- a corkscrew and bottle opener

- a tin opener

- an alarm clock

- a toilet roll

- any medicines you need, plus general medicines such as painkillers, plasters and contraception

- toiletries

- mobile phone

- laptop or personal computer

- lots of file paper and some files
- a dictionary and any general reference books
- pens, scissors, paper clips, a hole punch, correction fluid, rubber, etc
- contact details for family and friends
- towels (large and small)
- hairdryer
- coat hangers
- bedding – this may be provided but you may prefer to take your own and extra blankets
- clothes, shoes and underwear – take lots of outdoor clothing as you'll be spending more time waiting at bus stops and train stations and can't ring for a parental taxi any more!

'The way I worked out the basic things I needed was by thinking about what I did on a typical day, for example, what do I have in the morning? – toiletries, breakfast, etc. But I didn't anticipate quite how cold Edinburgh would be, so I didn't bring as many jumpers as I should have. When you are studying far from home it's better to bring too much stuff, because you can't pop home if you forget something.'

Samantha Northey, third-year Chinese student, Edinburgh University

If you have room for anything else then think about taking:

- portable music player
- plants
- posters and Blu-Tack
- photos
- ornaments
- games (Trivial Pursuit, etc)

- a TV (for which you'll need a licence)
- sports equipment
- an extension lead with circuit breaker.

Even if you're living in a hall where meals are provided take these basic cooking utensils as there'll be occasions when you miss meal times or don't feel like eating hall meals:

- two plates
- bowls
- knives, forks and spoons
- a medium-sized saucepan
- a wooden spoon
- a sharp knife
- a toaster.

If you're living in a self-catering hall, house or flat then you'll need these items in addition to those listed above:

- a large saucepan
- a frying pan
- a colander
- a spatula
- a cheese grater
- a measuring jug
- more cutlery
- more crockery
- an ovenproof dish
- recipe books
- more bedding, including lots of blankets or a duvet

- cleaning stuff for kitchens, bathrooms, floors, etc

- light bulbs

- a heater

- some basic DIY tools such as a hammer, screwdrivers (small and large), an adjustable spanner, pliers, nails and screws.

Insurance

This is essential even though money is tight (see *Making the pennies stretch*, page 81) particularly if you're taking expensive items, like a computer, mobile phone and MP3 player, as it will be really expensive to replace them. Why not ask a relative who always buys you presents you hate to buy you a year's insurance instead? **Endsleigh** is the student insurance specialist. If there isn't a branch at your university visit www.endsleigh.co.uk They can arrange for you to pay in instalments so you don't have to have all the money up front.

Sorting out money

It's a good idea to open up a student bank account before you start university – it's one less thing to do during freshers' week. The banks all start publishing their student deals from the late summer onwards in a bid for student business. Look in newspapers and on the internet for details, and pick the one that's offering the best deal. Be careful to look at everything that they are offering, as the one that has the best introductory offer may not also offer the best overdraft interest rates. Think about how you are going to use your bank account and pick one that suits your needs. Compare the different offers at the **National Association for Managers of Student Services'** website at www.support4learning.org.uk/money/banks.htm

Apply for an account in plenty of time so that you have all your cheque books and cards well before you leave.

There's more information about bank accounts in *Bank overdrafts*, page 71.

The first few days and weeks at university are always expensive, as you have to pay for lots of things that fall outside your day-to-day expenditure. So that you don't end up blowing your student loan in the first few weeks of term try to work during the summer to get sufficient funds to cover:

- university accommodation fees or deposit and first month's rent

- essential reading-list books

- getting to university

- joining clubs and societies

- going out during freshers' week

- stocking up with essential cupboard and/or housing items.

'I have got on very well with my bank. I have an overdraft facility which came automatically when I joined and it goes up by a small amount each year. They're always very helpful to me.'

Katrina Woods, second-year sociology student, Ulster University

---

Life skills

For many students, going to university is the first time they will have lived on their own and fended for themselves. It's as well to make sure that you have mastered the basics of looking after yourself before you fly the nest.

You will need to know how to:

- buy groceries on a budget

- make your own doctors, dentists and other medical appointments

- avoid getting suckered into signing up for store cards and credit cards

- wash and dry your clothes without shrinking them or turning them a different colour

- cook tasty meals that are good for you

- travel around without relying on a parental taxi

- carry out basic DIY repairs.

You will find tips throughout this book, but it's a good idea to make the most of your family and friends before you leave. Get them to help you with anything you feel unsure about. They will be happy to offer advice, and it may also help them get their heads around the fact that you are leaving home.

Saying goodbye

Leaving home is a difficult time for everyone. You may be looking forward to it, you may feel a bit scared, you may be worried about leaving your mates or a relationship. It's easy under these circumstances to forget that this change doesn't just affect you – it affects the people around you too. Your parents, brothers and sisters, relatives, friends and boyfriend or girlfriend are going to miss you and feel anxious about you moving away. Try to be sympathetic to their feelings and make time to listen to their concerns.

'It was a bit of a culture shock starting university. On the first day, when your parents leave you in your room with all your stuff just dumped there, it takes a while to sink in. But then you meet other people and talk to them, which takes your mind off things. Everybody else is in the same situation.'

**Phil Pearce, fifth-year business studies student,
Luton University**

It's important that you have the time and space to settle into your new environment without overly worrying about people at home. If you are constantly in touch with home and coming back for visits then you won't give yourself the opportunity to make new mates. This can make things very difficult further down the line when other people at uni have palled up. There's no easy answer – it's about trying to strike a balance. You may find these tips help.

Parents

- If possible let them drive you or come with you on your first day. This way they can see where you are living and working, and will find it easier to imagine you in your new surroundings.

- Arrange a regular time, at least once a week, when you'll call them to let them know how you are getting on. Call them even if things aren't going great – they will worry more if they don't hear from you at all.

Friends

- Talk to them about the things that you are looking forward to and the things you are anxious about – chances are a lot of you will be in the same boat at the same time.

- Tempting though it is to invite your mates down to stay with you in your new unsupervised surroundings, hold back for a few weeks. Give yourself the chance to meet other people at university first.

- Take their phone numbers and email addresses with you – that way you can stay in touch and let each other know how you are getting on. Hearing from a familiar person can be a great support.

- Try not to get too upset if some friendships drift – you will be making new friends too. And if you go back home in the holidays, you may find you are able to pick your friendship up again.

Boyfriends/girlfriends

Relationships are most difficult to know how to handle when going away to university. It may well be tempting to either apply for the same university or try to study in the same town. This can work, but the danger is that if you split up you will have the pain of watching your ex out with other people, while you have missed out on hooking up with all the gorgeous people you could have met in the first few weeks. However, long distance relationships require an equal commitment from both partners.

- Try to be honest with each other about how you feel and what you are scared of. If one of you isn't so committed it's probably best to call it quits so that you are both free to form other relationships.

- If staying together, then make a regular arrangement each day when you can have a proper chat without too many interruptions. If you know you won't be able to call at your arranged time let the other person know why, so they don't worry and become anxious.

- Send daily emails letting your partner know how you are getting on.

- After a few weeks invite them down to stay with you so they can meet your friends.

Your expectations

It's completely normal to become preoccupied about what university will be like – to spend time wondering about whether the other students will share your interests, if you will make friends, what your course will involve and if you will find the work easy or difficult.

The chances are that university will turn out to be partly like you imagine and partly very different. Having spent so much time imagining what it will be like, it can be difficult to deal with the things that are different. Try talking to other people in your halls or course about what they thought it would be like. What have been the surprises for them? Comparing notes can be very revealing, and you might end up having a good laugh about each other's preconceived ideas of uni.

However, if you find that your expectations aren't being met and you begin to feel anxious and upset about it then it's best to admit to how you are feeling. There are several people in universities and students' unions who can help under these circumstances. You'll find details of them in Chapter eight.

Chapter two
When you get there

This chapter covers:

- Queuing

- Enrolling

- Moving in

- Student loan

- Paying tuition fees

- Registering with your department

- Registering with the health service

- Library tours

- Looking for a job

- Entertainments

- Freshers' fairs

- Finding your way around

- Students' unions

- The National Union of Students

- Lifesavers

When you first arrive at university there can be a bewildering number of things to do all apparently at the same time. However, if you know what you have to do and work through your list then you will get there. Lots of activities will have been organised to help you settle in and get to know your fellow students.

Queuing

Although it can be daunting, it's better to go and register and sign up for things without your parents or any friends who have given you a lift to university. There is an awful lot of standing in queues involved as everyone else is doing the same rounds, but this is a really good opportunity to say hello to some of your fellow students. Ask them where they've come from, what they are studying and where they are going to be living. By the time you reach the front of the queue you may have met other students on your course or found out what other people's evening plans are. At the very least you will know a few people who you can smile and say hello to next time your paths cross – an invaluable asset in helping you feel at home in your new surroundings.

However, it's much more difficult to strike up a conversation with someone standing next to you if your parents or friends are there too. If they want to wait around and see you settled, suggest that you meet up later for a coffee when you can tell them how you've got on.

'It's strange because you speak to so many people and then if you see them later in the year, you don't quite know them and you don't know whether to say hello or not. I did make some good friends in the first week though.'

Katherine Lawrey, fourth-year Hispanic studies and history student, Birmingham University

---

Enrolling

Read the documents that you've got from the university carefully. In some institutions you will need to go to the accommodation office first to pick up your keys, while other universities ask you to go to the main hall or registrar's office to show your letter of acceptance and ID.

You'll be given a university card, which usually doubles as your library card. Over the next few days you'll acquire several cards, so make sure that you bring at least four passport-sized photographs with you as each card you're issued with will require one (see *Packing*, page 14).

Moving in

Once you have your keys you need to find out where your accommodation is. If you are given any security codes write them down and keep them with the rest of your documents – it can be another bonding process with your fellow students as you all try to work out how to get into your rooms for the first time.

You'll obviously need to move all your stuff into your room, and it will be tempting to set about making it feel like home immediately. However, it's best just to unpack the bare essentials – toiletries, any change of clothes and your stuff for making hot drinks – and then get on with all the other things you have to do before the end of the day.

If your hall or room has phone lines then you may need to go and sign a contract for them – get this out of the way. You will almost certainly be expected to attend a meeting if you are living in university accommodation where you find out about the house/hall rules, the fire procedures and meet your wardens and security staff.

If you have time, then unpack the rest of your things and set about making your room feel like home. Prop open your door while you are doing this, so you are not shut off from people and can see who your house-, flat- or hall-mates are.

Go into the communal kitchen and check what the arrangements are for allocating cupboards and storing food. Keep the bare minimum in student kitchens as food has a nasty habit of 'walking' late at night when hungry people return from pubs and clubs. While in the kitchen offer to put the kettle on and ask other people on your corridor or in your house whether they would like a cuppa. This is a great way of endearing yourself to your house- or hall-mates and getting to know those who you will be living with for the next year.

'If you smile and say hello to someone and they smile and say hello back then you've made a friend. Even if it is just a friend to whom you just smile and say hello. Some people will do more than smile and say hello and you'll have made a friend to go to the bar with or for a coffee.'

**Mona Lisa Cook, former welfare officer,
Loughborough University**

Don't worry if you don't get any further than the typical freshers' questions in the first few weeks: What's your name? Where do you come from? What A levels did you do? What course are you on? Talk to any student, past or present, and they'll recognise those questions. They're what all first-year students have in common, and are as good a starting point as any other. Use them if you're unsure about how to strike up a conversation.

Student loan

If your student loan application has gone smoothly then the first instalment should be transferred to your bank account on the first day of term. Any bursaries you have been awarded may also go straight into your bank account or may be paid as a cheque that you have to go to the finance office to collect.

If your student loan hasn't arrived try not to panic. Ask the finance office for help to find out what has happened to it and how to chase it. Most banks are sympathetic to student loans arriving late if you have the paperwork to prove that you have accepted your university place and are eligible for a student loan. Go to the nearest branch of your bank (or call them if you have internet banking), explain the situation and ask them for an overdraft.

Keep records of everything you are doing to chase up your student loan including emails, letters and phone calls. When making a phone call make sure you take a note of the name of the person you are speaking to, the date and time of the call and what is said or agreed. That way you can refer to it later or produce it as proof if needed.

Paying tuition fees

If you apply for a course in 2006 and start university in 2006/2007 or later then you will be able to apply for a student loan to cover any tuition fees you are liable for. You won't have to worry about handing over any money to the university. This will happen automatically when you are awarded the student loan to cover your tuition fees.

There's more information about student loans and tuition fees in Chapter four.

Registering with your department

At some point during the first week you will be given a time to go and register with your department. This may be on the first day or you may be given a couple of days to settle in.

Registering with your department is often the first chance you get to meet the other people on your course as you are likely to be all standing in a queue again. These are the people who will be going through the same highs and lows as you for at least the next three years. Make a big effort to say hello and introduce yourself. That way you will have some familiar faces to gravitate towards when you walk into your first lecture or tutorial.

When you register you will be given your:

- timetable and syllabus

- a map of the department's lecture halls, tutorial rooms, labs, etc

- email addresses for getting in touch with your tutors and your university email address

- information about any introductory talks or courses

- information about how to choose and select any options.

'We had an induction module week before the beginning of term. It was like normal lectures but more informal. The members of the department introduced themselves to us, told us their specialities, gave us information about the course, our timetables and so on. They also told us about a drinks party in a pub where we could get to know them and the students in other years. It was a really good way to be introduced.'

Martin Petchey, second-year psychology student, Luton University

You will also be given details of a departmental social event where you get to meet all your tutors informally. It's a really good idea to go to these events. Try to introduce yourself to most, if not all, of the tutors who are teaching the courses you are taking. Make a particular point of introducing yourself to your personal tutor, if you have been allocated one already. And don't knock back too much of the free booze!

'I met my personal tutor in the first week of the first year. This was brilliant because in my tutor group there were five of us and we instantly had a connection – we were all doing the same course and had the same tutor and in the first week of university that is all you need to be firm friends.'

Elizabeth Hardaker, fourth-year biology masters student, University of Bath

Registering with the health service

This is something that students often put off in the maelstrom of the first few days. However, a surprising number of freshers get ill during this time, and it's much easier to sort out registering with a new doctor or health centre before you are feeling like death warmed up.

Your university will probably have sent you details of local doctors' surgeries and health centres that have vacancies for university students or there will be a student health centre just for your campus. If you can't find the details ask at the registrar's office or accommodation office.

You will need to take your NHS medical card to the surgery and fill out their forms. You will then be able to make appointments to see the doctor.

If you do need medical treatment before you are registered then most doctors will see you as an emergency patient or you can get treatment at the accident and emergency department of the local hospital.

If there isn't a dentist in your student health centre, then you will have to register with a local practice. Your university should provide details and you normally just have to go and register by filling in some forms.

There's more information in Chapter eight.

Library tours

You will usually be offered tours of the library and other study facilities the university has in the first few days. It might not seem like a priority at the time, particularly if you've been partying hard, but you should definitely go to these. You will save an awful lot of time later if you know where to go for your books, public internet access, language labs, workshops, studios, laboratories, etc., how you get access to them and how things are organised, including any passwords and security codes you need.

Looking for a job

If you know you are going to need to work during term time (see *Making the pennies stretch*, page 81) then you need to ask about local job opportunities when you first get to university. Students' unions employ students in bars, shops, cafes and to help out with entertainments, etc. These are often sorted out on a first come first served basis. Ask at your students' union office or check out the union noticeboard or intranet for details. Your students' union may also be able to point you in the direction of other local job opportunities.

There's more information in Chapter five.

Entertainments

'My freshers' week was good. We have an introduction-week card for which you pay £25 but then entry to everything is free during that week. There was a huge variety to choose from, a lot of different music to account for all tastes. You could even go and see Timmy Mallet!'

Susanna Craig, first-year politics and parliamentary studies student, Leeds University

Your students' union will have organised at least one event, and more likely a series of events, to help you meet other students. The nature of freshers' events depends entirely upon the imagination and energy of the people running your students' union and can range from organised quiz and game shows to spontaneous pub crawls. Try to avoid events that aren't organised by the union as they may be a rip-off. Go to at least one of the university events, even if you're unsure about meeting new people. The later you leave it, the harder it will be to make friends because people will have begun to form groups. Remember that initially everybody is in the same position and will be as nervous as each other, even if some are better at hiding it.

'It was more a freshers' few days than a week but it was good, if a bit daunting. I don't think you should panic if your freshers' week is disappointing because it doesn't mean the rest will be bad – there's lots more to come. If I were to choose my top five nights out at uni, none of them would be from freshers' week.'

Katherine Lawrey, fourth-year Hispanic studies and history student, Birmingham University

Most students' unions organise a freshers' ball. These aren't usually formal affairs but all-night parties with a mixture of live music, discos and extended bar licences. They may be held towards the end of the freshers' introduction period and be open to students from other years. This is a very good way of getting to meet other students at the university. Although you might also want to be on the lookout for predatory second and third years – don't feel pressurised into doing anything you don't want to just in a bid to fit in.

Freshers' fairs

Freshers' fairs – sometimes also known as intro fairs, or even 'faires' in those universities with 'olde worlde' pretensions – are where you can find out about all the university's clubs and societies. There'll also be other organisations there anxious to attract your custom, ranging from the Armed Forces to the local cinema, and banks to magazines. They'll all be handing out freebies to grab your attention. Find the one that's giving away the largest plastic bag and make sure you get all the freebies you can – that packet of instant pasta sauce may not seem that appealing at the time, but you will find a use for it.

'I went to the freshers' fair and looked at all the societies (and took the freebies!) and then went back to the ones I was interested in – the photography society and the film society. I only joined two because I wanted to see how my workload would pan out first and how much free time I would have. Also, they ask for money there and then when you join and I didn't have enough to join more!'

**Katie Hogan, first-year sociology student,
Essex University**

Most universities offer an impressive range of sports and extracurricular activities and there is bound to be something that interests you. But be wary of over enthusiastic club members trying hard to persuade you to join – you may have to pay a fee to join. Look at the complete list of stalls and set yourself a limit before joining anything. Your students' union may publish a handbook giving you more details about the clubs' or societies' past history, successes and meeting times. Clubs and societies are great places to meet people with whom you share a common interest, but if you're asked for money find out where it goes and what you get for it.

Finding your way around

Some universities run tours of the local area, when you'll be shown the student haunts and the places to avoid. In some towns there can be friction between students and the local community, while in others the relationship is harmonious or the student population just gets absorbed into the crowds. You'll be warned by your students' union if there's an antagonistic relationship between locals and students. Read Chapter eleven for ways to avoid trouble and tactics to keep you safer.

'My university has three sites so it was difficult to find my way around to start with. I still don't know all the parts to it, but that's not a problem because we generally go as a group when we have to go to an area we haven't been to before.'

Vicky Spencer, third-year textile design student, Chelsea College of Art and Design

If you aren't offered a tour then explore for yourself with other students. If you're living in a self-catering hall or house then you'll have to do this almost as soon as you get there, as you'll need to learn quickly where to buy cheap food. Ask students already at the university where the best local shops are and if there are any markets where you can buy food cheaply (see also *Healthy eating*, page 153).

While it can appear daunting at first to familiarise yourself with a new area when you have so much else going on, it's worth doing. Everywhere has something else to offer other than just the local university campus activities, and you're likely to gain a great deal from exploring your nearest town's social, cultural and culinary life. Many students find that they like the town where they go to university so much that they never leave!

Get a guide book to get you started. *Rough Guides* produce city guides to most areas where there are universities in England, Northern Ireland, Scotland and Wales. Look out for them in book shops or visit www.roughguides.com

'A couple of times every week a few of us would go off campus and explore the local area. This generally meant finding a new pub for lunch. By the time we knew where all the pubs were we could navigate the local area fairly easily.'

Andrew Stephenson, third-year business management student, Royal Holloway College, University of London

Students' unions

It can be very confusing when you first get to university to get your head round what students' unions do. This is because their activities are so varied. They offer a wealth of advice and support on things like accommodation, money, jobs, work, travelling around – in fact anything that you might come across while at university. In most cases they should be your first port of call for any advice you need or any problems you encounter.

'My JCR, which is what our students' union is known as, has supported me completely and assisted me a lot even when it wasn't their responsibility. There is an extremely good internal student atmosphere. I ended up getting actively involved and was elected onto the JCR as a policy adviser to the president on disability and welfare.'

Tony Leighton, theology and philosophy of religion student, Oxford University

In addition to sorting out problems they also provide much of the fun things too like the bars, cafes, entertainments, clubs and societies. Often these are run on a subsidised basis so that they are affordable for impoverished students.

Most students' unions are members of the **National Union of Students (NUS)** too and if yours is then you can pick up an NUS card, which will also help make your life more affordable. Show an NUS card to get discounts at cinemas, art galleries, theatres, travel agents, some clothes shops and many other outlets. More details are on www.nusonline.co.uk Activate your card online to get access to even more discounts. You can also take advantage of the NUS's publications, advice, information and training services.

Sports and socs

Don't risk missing out on all that university can offer you by just studying and finding a regular spot at the bar. University offers you a really valuable opportunity to try out new things and gain skills to offer to future employers. This is vital in an age when a university degree is not an automatic passport to a job of your choice. University clubs and societies (socs) provide excellent opportunities to develop new skills while having fun and making friends who share your interests. See also Chapter twelve.

'I decided to join the badminton club. I've made loads of friends and had a good laugh playing the sport I enjoy. We are in the BUSA league (the university sports league), which has meant that we meet loads of people from around the country, compete against them and make friends further afield.'

**Paul Blundell, first-year psychology student,
Lincoln University**

There will be numerous sports clubs and socs to choose from. The best time to join is at your freshers' fair (see *Freshers' fairs*, page 31). All clubs and socs will have a stand and at least one enthusiastic member keen to sign you up. If you miss joining the activity of your choice at the freshers' fair, then contact it through the pigeon holes in the students' union or by email. You'll usually be able to join at any point during the year.

Most sports clubs cater for all levels of experience, from complete beginners to well advanced. If you want to play sport seriously at university contact the club as soon as possible, as trials tend to be held in the first few weeks of term.

If there isn't a club or a society that caters for your interest then you could set one up. Go to the students' union officer with responsibility for sports and/or societies. The rules vary, but usually you'll have to collect signatures from people who are also interested, outline how it would be run and present this to the committee that allocates budgets. If it's approved you'll be given some money and be up and running! It will then be down to you to keep it going and present financial reports.

'My first impressions were that university was full of people that conformed to student stereotypes. First impressions were misleading though, and I soon found a group of people I love through doing plays in the drama society.'

**Peter Rodger, second-year biology student,
Wentworth College, University of York**

Ents and events

Entertainments and events is probably the area that most students get involved with. What's offered will depend entirely on where you're studying but 'ents' are a big part of all students' unions. Some unions have excellent reputations as gig venues where you can see up-and-coming bands cheaply. Other unions focus on getting local bands in and running regular discos. You can also see plays, cabaret, listen to classical music and take part in quiz nights in your union.

If you want to have a say in the entertainments run by your union find out whether there's an ents committee. This plans and books acts with the help of a member of staff and/or sabbatical officer. This can be very popular so be quick if you're interested. There can be certain perks to being an ents officer, such as free gig passes, but you'll probably also find yourself cleaning up the mess long after most people have gone to bed!

Rag

Rag is extremely big in some unions and includes all the wild and wacky events students' unions run to raise money for charities. You will be hounded at some point and asked to do anything from a three-legged pub crawl, to sitting on a bed in your PJs while being wheeled down the high street. Medical students have a particularly strong reputation (deservedly so) for insane rag antics.

Most universities have an annual rag week. Pick up a rag mag that lists everything that's going on and there may be a rag ball. Even the faint-hearted have been known to throw themselves into rag week and there's usually a fantastic atmosphere on campus. Other universities collect throughout the year, get tons of students involved and raise huge amounts of money. It's a winning combination of having lots of fun while doing some good and making a difference.

Student community action

This is growing in universities around the country. Students volunteer to help people in the local community, doing anything from helping in homes for the elderly to running youth and school projects. It's a great way of getting to know your local community better and opening your mind to life outside the closed world of university. Ask your union whether it has such a scheme.

Student media

All universities have their own student newspaper or magazine. These may have a sabbatical editor or be run entirely by full-time students. Student newspapers and magazines are a fantastic way for budding journos to get practical experience – in fact anyone who has ambitions in this area and doesn't sign up will be asked by future employers why not. Media jobs are probably the most competitive and you'll need to be able to demonstrate practical experience. Even people considering you for work experience placements will be more likely to use you if you can show an interest. Student publications aren't just for writers either – subeditors, photographers, designers, website bods, cartoonists and illustrators, even meteorologists – may all be welcome. If you think you've got something to offer, offer it and see what they say.

You may also find that your uni has a radio or television station. Again, great for gaining experience. Student radio stations are increasing, but if there isn't one at your university try offering your services to the local hospital radio.

Getting involved

You can get involved with your students' union at many levels – from attending a union general meeting, where union policy is debated, to standing for election onto a committee. Don't be put off if you find it difficult to follow the first meeting you attend. The detail of regulations which govern them can be confusing for even the most seasoned union officer, but it won't be long before you can sort through the jargon enough to follow the proceedings.

Most unions allow any student of the university to attend the general meetings – in fact they positively welcome you with open arms. Any committee positions will be well advertised in the union buildings. You'll need to get a nomination form signed and draw up a manifesto. You then attend the electoral meeting and make a short speech outlining your ideas and beliefs. After that it's up to the meeting whether you're elected to that position or not.

If you really want to have a say in how your union is run then you can stand for one of the sabbatical positions. Each students' union has a number of sabbatical officers or 'sabbs' – the number of them will vary according to the size of the university. Sabbs are students who have been elected by the annual general meeting of students. They are then paid a salary for a year to do the job they were elected to. Generally, sabbatical officers are responsible for education matters, welfare, representation, sports, societies, entertainments and the finances of the union. Some student newspapers also have sabbatical editors.

'I have gained a wealth of experience from getting involved in my students' union, such as managing a budget and organising big events. The experience has been very rewarding and I have got to meet loads of new people. I would recommend that everyone get involved in their students' union.'

Andrew Stephenson, third-year business management student, Royal Holloway College, University of London

To find the contact details of students' unions around the country log onto www.studentunion.co.uk where you will find students' unions grouped into geographical areas and then listed alphabetically.

The National Union of Students

If your university is a member of the **National Union of Students (NUS)** – and most of them are – then you'll automatically become a member. If you study in Wales, Scotland or Northern Ireland then you become a member of the UCMC, NUS Scotland or NUS Northern Ireland respectively. There are also regional branches that supply these services on a more localised basis.

The NUS represents students' views to national and Government organisations. It holds one conference a year where national policies are set and elections held. Your NUS regional branch will also have an annual conference to elect its officers and set local policy. If you want to get involved with the NUS and help decide on campaigns and policies then ask your own students' union president or contact the NUS at www.nusonline.co.uk

Lifesavers

It's not uncommon to have problems in the first few days. There's an awful lot to do, all in unfamiliar surroundings, and a host of problems can crop up. If you do have a problem then don't be tempted just to keep quiet. Tell the relevant person at your university. If you are unsure about who this is then ask your students' union or welfare services for advice.

Chapter three
Down to work

This chapter covers:

- Successful study
- Different types of courses
- Teaching
- Research and resources
- Presenting coursework
- Winning essays
- Passing exams
- Changing course
- Lifesavers

You are making a hefty financial commitment to your university course, and most people want to do well. Much of doing well at university is about being organised and methodical, asking for guidance and more information when you need it, and using your time effectively. If you also remember that your tutors want you to do well too and are there to help you, and you don't let things build up to the point where you feel you can't cope, then you should be fine.

'I felt daunted about work because you are left to your own devices. But it's OK to feel that way because at the same time it's exciting. At the end of the first year, when you have passed the exams, you can say "I did this." '

Samantha Northey, third-year Chinese student, Edinburgh University

Successful study

University tutors treat you as an adult. They assume you're motivated to find out more about your subject and are interested in it. It's left largely up to you to select the material to complete your coursework. You'll be given suggested reading lists and websites, but will no longer be told which sources you 'need' to consult. Adjusting to this way of teaching may take some time, but there are things you can do to help you through.

'There's no one there to push you at university. They'll just kick you off the course rather than chase you for an essay. Having said that, they are very helpful if you go and ask them. I've found that my lecturers are always willing to help.'

Peter Rodger, second-year biology student, Wentworth College, University of York

Get organised

Your department should publish a course guide which tells you what topics will be covered, what skills and competencies you are expected to demonstrate, how you will be assessed and which pieces of work count towards your final marks. Keep this document somewhere safe and make sure you keep referring to it – having this basic information will make it much easier to organise yourself. Always ask your tutor or departmental secretary if you're unclear about what is expected from you.

Managing your time

Some universities run introductory study sessions on time management, which include a tour of the study facilities and can be extremely useful. Time management is essential to studying effectively while not going over the top. Work out:

- where you're supposed to be and when

- which courses require you to do background reading or preparation

- which tutors want work from you, what it is and when you have to hand it in.

Plan your weekly work schedule around this information. Don't set yourself unrealistic work schedules – it will only depress you when you fail to keep up with them. And don't work for excessively long periods of time. How long you can concentrate for is up to you to discover, but a general guideline is to try working for 40 minutes and relaxing for 10 or 20 minutes. When you do stop, don't feel guilty and make sure you relax properly. Have a cup of coffee, read the papers or flop in front of the television for a while. No one expects you to work all the time.

Make lists of what you have to do by certain dates – it's very therapeutic to cross things off a list once you have completed them. Order these lists into 'urgent' tasks, 'necessary' tasks and those which can be left until last. If you find that your list is heavily weighted on the 'urgent' side then you're not planning your time well. Reorganise things to give yourself more realistic time schedules.

If you have particular difficulties organising your workload then try keeping a diary for a week. Write down everything you do during the day, honestly, then look back on it and see where you've wasted time, where you've used time efficiently and where you needed to relax more. Then rearrange your schedule around this information.

'At some point during your university career you have to make a decision about what sort of degree you want. University is not only about the piece of paper you emerge with. Most people can get a 2.1 or a 2.2 without knocking themselves out and leave themselves time to do other things.'

Phil Agulnik, former University of London Union President

Use your fellow students

Your fellow students are a valuable study aid. Comparing notes and talking about difficulties is very helpful. It's much easier to solve a problem if there are several brains tackling it, and you'll get a broader view of your course by comparing ideas.

However, you need to strike the right balance. Don't feel pressurised into working at an accelerated rate just to try to keep up with the class swot. Nor should you feel pressurised to 'slack off' because other people don't seem to be doing as much work – they probably are, behind closed doors.

Your work area

Where you choose to work is very much up to you. Some people like working in a library where everything is quiet and books are to hand. Other people feel happier working in a more familiar environment and can cope with lots of background noise.

'My best advice is work in the library if you can. Trying to work in your room is a nightmare, particularly when living off campus in your second year. There are so many distractions. You'll get far more done and then can have a break and not feel guilty about it.'

Peter Rodger, second-year biology student, Wentworth College, University of York

Wherever you work, make sure you keep the area tidy and organised as this saves huge amounts of time. You really don't want to be rummaging through piles of paper to find the relevant sources for your coursework, when you have to hand it in at the end of the day.

Filing

Stay on top of your coursework with a good filing system. For paperwork, opt for a filing case with lots of suspended folders so you can organise your papers into relevant topics and modules. These don't take up much room and come in plastic, metal and cardboard. Label the folders clearly so you can quickly find the relevant papers.

You will also need to create good electronic filing systems. Use consistent file names so that you can locate your documents easily. The fewer files that you have in each folder the easier it is to find things so use separate folders for each course or module. Then create subfolders for each essay topic, presentation or practical assessment. Take time to make sure you save your work in the right place. File the course emails that you want to keep in folders that are called by the same names as those for your word-processed documents. Do the same with the 'folders' option under 'internet favourites' for any URLs you want to keep to refer back to.

Backing up

Even in the twenty-first century, technology can go wrong. Protect yourself from your computer crashing and eating the essay you have just spent four days writing by making sure that you back up everything regularly. It's as well to keep copies of all your folders as well as your recent coursework. Invest in a CD writer if your PC doesn't have one – they don't cost much and could save hours, days or even months of precious work.

If you produce work on the university's computers then ask what back-up facilities they have and what systems there are for retrieving lost data. And it sounds very obvious, but do make sure that you save everything that you are working on regularly.

Different types of courses

At most universities you will study for a Bachelor of Arts or a Bachelor of Science degree known as an honours degree. These are usually studied as single honours, where you do one subject, and joint honours, where you study two subjects that carry equal weight when it comes to assessment and examination. In England, Wales and Northern Ireland most honours degrees take three years, and in Scotland they are studied over four years.

Increasingly, degree courses are taught in 'modules', which allow you to pick from a wide range of topics within your area of study and even from subjects within other departments. This allows you to really choose topics that interest you, although you need to bear in mind how your choice will come across to future employers.

'My tip is to stick to whole units unless there is a course you especially want to study which is only run as a half unit. There's definitely more work involved in doing two half units. Lecturers treat half units as full unit courses and expect you to do as much preparation for the classes. I had to write six assessed essays for my full unit and ten for my two half units.'

Phil Agulnik, former University of London Union President

You have to be well organised when following a modular degree as you can't be late handing in essays. Your essays have to be consistently good, and your attendance at lectures, seminars and tutorials is often part of your assessment. Ask for advice from your tutors and take your time when choosing options.

'Don't leave assessed work to the last minute the way I do! Consult with lecturers if you can because they can give useful advice about what they are looking for in the work. Use the library, which has a lot of information if you take the time to look, and the internet is also a good resource.'

Rhian Jones, fourth-year European studies and French student, Manchester University

Placement courses

Some courses require a short work placement or an exchange, which is not directly assessed but is intended to give you an idea of how your degree can be used in the outside world. These are usually arranged at the beginning of your second year. Your tutors will give you information about firms that offer such placements or help you to arrange your own.

Sandwich courses

Sandwich courses usually involve a year's work placement in an industry connected with your degree before your final year. You can make other arrangements, however, such as working for the four summer terms or during holidays. The placement is regarded as a full-time job, and you may be paid a good wage. On the other hand, you may not be so lucky and end up being used as cheap labour. Talk to your tutors about the reputation of the firm you'll be working for. Tutors can also suggest firms you can approach for your sandwich-year placement. If you're a sponsored student then you'll probably do your placement with the firm that is sponsoring you. (See also *Sponsorship*, page 74.)

'My course arranged a place in industry for me. I worked in Luton and I'm still in contact with the company, I'm doing a mini-project for them at the moment. You learn a lot in your year out that you can put into practice later in your modules. The disadvantages are that when you come back all your friends have graduated, which can be tough.'

Phil Pearce, fifth-year business studies student, Luton University

Your work will be assessed while you're on placement and your employer asked for a written report on your performance. You have to do a detailed project that is part of your final degree mark. If you sign up for sandwich courses and then can't find a placement, talk to your department.

Courses in Scotland

Courses in Scotland last for four years. The first year is spent studying your main subject together with one closely related to it, and a subject of your own choice that can be completely unrelated to your main subject. The Scottish degree structure means you get the chance to study various subjects you're interested in before making your final decision.

'You start off on one course but at the end of the first year you can change courses as long as you do well in the exams – it's not set in stone from the beginning. In England there is less flexibility. I suppose a disadvantage could be that you graduate later than your friends in other areas of the UK but that doesn't bother me.'

Samantha Northey, third-year Chinese student, Edinburgh University

Studying abroad

Increasingly, you can study abroad and not just if you're doing languages. The European Union has led to many universities including language or overseas study into their courses. There are also European schemes such as Erasmus and Tempus that help meet the costs of living and studying abroad. Full details will be available from your university.

Language students will usually be offered the choice of studying at a university, teaching in a school as an assistant or doing a work placement during their year abroad. However, you may be able to arrange alternatives as long as you can demonstrate you are going to do more than just hang out in the local bars and cafes. Speak to your department about your options.

'Try to get in touch with the student who had your placement previously – they can help a lot. Don't worry if you don't enjoy your first month; that's normal. It gets easier as you settle in.'

Isabelle Brewerton, fourth-year modern and medieval languages student, Corpus Christi College, Cambridge University

Teaching

Teaching in universities is far less personal than the tuition you'll have received at school. You have to rely on your own initiative to a greater extent and be prepared to collate your own information.

You will also be expected to attend your classes. Don't think that just because there are lots more people in your classes you won't be noticed. Universities check attendance. Any absences must be explained to the departmental secretary or tutor. If you are ill you are expected to contact them in advance. If you have a poor attendance record then you could be penalised and made to sit the unit again, not be given a mark for that course or even asked to leave.

'At university there's no-one constantly nagging you if you don't do the work, so you need self-motivation. I've realised that the only person I could disappoint is myself. Your days are less structured and you have to organise your time yourself, whereas at school you had lesson time then homework time.'

Jennifer Hogan, fourth-year natural sciences student, Clare College, Cambridge University

---

Lectures

Lectures are talks given by tutors to a large group of students. You take your own notes and have to sign an attendance list to prove you were there. There's not much opportunity for discussion and debate. If you're an arts student then much of your course will be covered by lectures.

Some people find it difficult to adjust to this form of teaching. Any reading you do in advance helps you feel more confident in a sea of unfamiliar faces and subjects. Your lecture subjects are posted on departmental noticeboards and/or emailed to you. Some examinations are based on what's been covered in lectures. Find out if this is the case for your course as you'll have to take comprehensive notes to help you revise.

There is an art to taking notes and everybody develops his or her own style. General tips, though, are to write down key ideas rather than whole sentences, leave lots of space on the paper so that you can add things later, and use headings to give your notes some structure. It's unrealistic to think you can go through your notes in detail after each lecture and turn them into beautifully crafted pieces of English. However, 10 or 15 minutes filling in the blanks immediately after the lecture, when the information is still fresh in your mind, can make a big difference.

Lab work

If you're studying a non-humanities subject then a large part of your course is taught through laboratory work. You'll have more timetabled hours than arts students and will spend a great deal of your time in laboratories. You have to work on your own initiative and take responsibility for your own experiments.

Follow the instructions for the experiment carefully. Make sure you complete each stage. Keep an eye on the time and try not to overrun. Record your results neatly and efficiently. Leave yourself time to write up your conclusion.

Ask your tutors about how they want you to record and present your results. If you feel nervous about tackling practicals then do a bit of background reading first so you have a rough idea of what to expect. Get to your practical on time so you are guaranteed to get all the equipment you need. If you are working in groups or pairs then share the work out equally, so you don't end up 'carrying' one member of the group who you then have to explain everything to later.

Fieldwork

If your course includes fieldwork then you might spend quite a bit of time out of the classroom. You may also be expected to go on two or three major field expeditions. These usually take place during the vacations, so can affect your holiday or money earning plans. You may also have to do a fieldwork project under your own initiative for your final degree result. Your department will usually offer several alternatives, or you can arrange your own project with your tutor.

Generally, fieldwork is fun and a good way of bonding with your fellow students. Make sure you are organised about making notes and recording your results, as you will have to write everything up at the end. If you make careful notes, drawings, photographs and statistics out in the field you won't have to go back over things at the end of the day, and will have more time to join in with the social activities that usually form some part of the fieldwork expedition.

'I've done a lot of fieldwork on my course, which usually involves going somewhere for the afternoon or a whole day and studying the particular topic we are covering on the course. It's extremely varied. You can elect to go abroad, but that costs extra. But wherever you go take a waterproof! And be organised. Don't just scribble your notes because it is raining and you want to rush. Lay them out properly or else you won't have a clue what you've written when you get back.'

**Allan Jones, third-year geography student,
Lancaster University**

Seminars

Seminars are discussions between a smaller group of students, with a tutor present to guide the proceedings. They can be extremely useful, particularly if the group is vocal and forthcoming with its ideas. They are an increasingly common way of teaching.

You may be asked to write a paper for one of your seminars and present it to the class. The content of a seminar paper is the same as that of an essay, but you'll have to present it in a different way. Stick to the same structure as you would for an essay – an introduction, discussion broken down into short points and a conclusion. But remember that your audience will be listening to you rather than reading your essay, so make your points clearly and concisely, linking them with a logical thread. Don't be daunted by speaking in front of your class – you'll all have to do it at some point. Most students find it's a valuable experience.

Remember to speak slowly taking deep breaths, and if you lose track of what you're saying just pause and gather your thoughts. If your mind goes completely blank, then ask someone in the group where you had got to – this is also a good way of testing whether they were listening!

Tutorials

You will meet your tutor on a one-to-one basis or in a small group to discuss specific topics, your essays and/or practicals. They are likely to be weekly or fortnightly events. Tutorials are probably the most valuable periods of teaching time you have, particularly if you get on well with your tutor. Make the most of them by doing any preparation or essays in time.

Don't be afraid to speak out. Contrary to what you might think tutors don't know everything, and you may come up with a point of view they hadn't considered before. Airing your ideas is also the best way to learn what is pertinent to your course. Don't be afraid of being wrong – if you knew everything there was to know about your subject you wouldn't need to be at university would you?

'I met my lecturers by them lecturing me. But as the sizes of the classes have got smaller I am now able to say 'Hi' to most of them. However, if I had needed them much in the first year I would have had a few problems, because I was very nervous of looking stupid.'

Elizabeth Hardaker, fourth-year biology masters student, University of Bath

Personal tutors

Your personal tutor is the person you should talk to if you have any problems that might have repercussions for your studies. The earlier your department knows about problems, the sooner it will be able to help you. You don't have to give any personal details – broad outlines will do. Universities are usually very accommodating providing you tell them what's wrong. If you really don't fancy talking to anyone in your department, then go to your students' union, who can act as mediators.

'We got a student guide for each course that gave us the email addresses for everyone teaching that course – tutors and lecturers – and departmental contacts. As for my personal tutor, I had to look up his contact details on the board at the union and arrange a meeting. It's not a bad system, but it would have been good to have had a face-to-face meeting with your personal tutor set up for you.'

Alastair Lee, first-year art and social sciences student, Dundee University

Research and resources

At university you are responsible for doing your own research. You will be given certain pointers during your tutorials and lectures about what resources to use, but you need to get to know what your university has to offer. Some universities have extensive facilities, while others may have reciprocal arrangements with other universities or central facilities that you can join. You should be told about the facilities during freshers' week, but always ask your department or tutors if you're unclear. If you have any particular requirements then make sure you ask your university about the provisions they have in place and any help they can give you to obtain specialist equipment.

'I said I was dyslexic at my interview and was told about the Language and Learning Centre here. They meet you when you start so that they can help you with your specific needs because everybody's are different. Things generally take longer to do than for most people, but the lecturers are lenient when they are aware of the situation. I always put a cover sheet on my essays to remind them.'

Claire Baldwin, third-year history student, Aberystwyth University

The library

You're likely to spend quite a few days in the library so it's important to learn how to use it effectively. First suss out the classification system as it may well be different from your school and local library. Books are usually classified by subject matter, but you'll be told how the system in your university works and how to find out about the availability of books. Also ask about fines! Some books will be for reference only, so you can't take them out at all, and others that are much in demand may be offered on a short-term loan basis only, incurring hefty fines – £1 a day is not uncommon. On your student loan you don't want extra costs like that.

'One of the lessons new students need to learn really quickly is that it's essential to go and get any references given during a lecture or tutorial immediately. If you don't go to the library for a couple of days then everyone else on the course has been there before and you can't do your assignment.'

Phil Agulnik, former University of London Union President

The photocopier is a useful piece of library equipment to get to know as it is very much cheaper to use than those in commercial shops. But beware of copyright law as it's illegal to copy more than a small amount from any one book. Check with your librarian before you copy anything from a book, published or not. If your department suspects you of copying from a book or from another student, you may be in danger of failing your degree.

Some large universities have a special 'past papers' area where you can look back on past examination papers for your course. The library will also house past students' dissertations and theses, which you can use as sources of information. Remember to credit the author, as copyright law applies as much to other students' work as it does to books.

Many libraries run video, CD and DVD rental services. The rules are likely to be different from those governing books, so do check – bringing back a DVD the following day may not be possible if you have to travel halfway across town to a player.

Technology labs

You will find much of the information required to complete your assignments online. You will also need access to email and have to hand-in your assignments as word-processed documents. You should have any databases that relate to your courses explained to you at the start of that course, and your lecturers and tutors will suggest relevant internet sites during your lectures and tutorials.

Some halls have internet access in each room, while other universities have large technology labs where you can surf the net. You can also use these labs if you don't have your own computer. Find out when they are open and what access codes you need. There are times when these facilities are much in demand, and you may have to wait or make an appointment so don't leave things to the very last minute.

If your university offers IT training courses then take them! One thing you can be sure of when you graduate is that you will need computer skills, and IT training outside is extremely expensive.

'There are special areas on campus called 'green card areas' which are extra computer rooms just for people with special needs, such as dyslexia or partial sight. That way we can always have access to a computer for our work.'

**Claire Baldwin, third-year history student,
Aberystwyth University**

Language labs

Language labs house audio equipment for aural language assignments, satellite TV, videos, DVDs and overseas native language newspapers.

Workshops and studios

You will have access to workshops and studios if there is a creative practical element to your course. These provide the specialist equipment you require. Make sure you find out when you can use them – the arrangements are usually flexible, but there will be security measures in place as universities want to protect their expensive equipment. Your departmental secretary will be able to tell you the rules.

Books

There are certain course books you need to buy. Ask your tutors which ones they'd recommend. Find out if your university has a second-hand bookshop or book exchange programme. Check noticeboards to see if any students are selling their old textbooks, and look at online booksellers like Amazon for special deals or 'used' offers. Then, and only then, visit your nearest bookshop and hand over a chunk of your student loan for a new copy. Although, unfortunately, there will be some courses, such as medicine, where this may not work and you may have to get the most recent edition.

See also *Making the pennies stretch*, page 81.

Presenting coursework

It's no good spending a great deal of time researching your topic if you then don't present it properly. You will lose marks for sloppy presentation and poor English.

Word processing

You will be expected to hand in all written work as a word-processed document. If you don't have your own computer then make sure you leave enough time to type your essay up during the hours that the university computer rooms are open – most will close at some point in the evening. Check what style guidelines your department likes – you may be given information about the font that they want you to use and things like the margins and line spacing. If they don't tell you this then use your own judgement, but steer clear of lots of formatting or fancy fonts. Times New Roman and Arial are the most commonly used fonts. And don't expect your tutors to squint at your work – choose an 11- or 12-point font size. Leave generous margins and 1.5 line spacing so that they have room to write their notes. Print your coursework out on plain paper and keep it all together in a plain folder.

Good English

However beautifully your work is presented, you are going to lose marks if it contains lots of spelling and grammar mistakes. You can't rely on spellcheckers to pick them all up, and your carefully constructed argument will be ruined by lots of basic errors. This means that you need to read all of your work through thoroughly before you hand it in. Most people find that they spot more things if they print it out to read rather than doing this on screen. And keep a dictionary to hand to check anything that you aren't sure about.

Winning essays

Every student has to submit essays – some courses require more than others, admittedly, but you won't be able to escape. Here are a few tips to get you going.

Research is the most time-consuming part of writing an essay, so begin your reading well in advance of the deadline. You won't be able to get away with just replicating the notes you take from your tutors' presentations. At university you are expected to draw your arguments from a variety of sources, and it will be even more impressive if you don't only use those that you are told about during your lectures. Use your library and the internet to gather relevant books and research. Make a note of those books and sources you refer to as you go along, as it is more difficult to remember where you got a piece of information later. Never, ever use people's words or research without acknowledging them. This is plagiarism and is taken very seriously, sometimes leading to expulsion.

'Do the reading in advance, that way even if you are writing the essay at the last minute you know what you are talking about. And don't build essays up. If you have, say, three to do in a term then do them one after the other. Don't leave them all to the end of term otherwise you go nuts with the pressure.'

Allan Jones, third-year geography student, Lancaster University

Getting started

Starting is often the hardest part. Read the question carefully several times – more marks are lost by students not answering the question than because of their lack of knowledge of the topic. Then type or write down your first thoughts – don't worry about constructing an argument, just make sure that you are not staring at a blank piece of paper. Then group your thoughts into an essay plan.

'I would say that the biggest obstacle is starting – it's not half as bad as you think once you put pen to paper or finger to keyboard.'

Jennifer Hogan, fourth-year natural sciences student, Clare College, Cambridge University

An essay plan should contain:

- what the introduction should say

- headings for the paragraphs that will form the main argument of your essay, and what you will discuss under each

- your conclusion, in which you sum up the main points you have made and present your opinion.

You then write your essay by 'filling in the blanks' in your essay plan and adding your references and bibliography. Footnotes are generally used to give the source of the quotations and information from other sources you have used. A bibliography is a comprehensive list of books you have used to research your essay. You may find that each department has stylistic preferences for how you present this information. Be consistent and don't swap between styles in an essay. And don't leave any references or books out.

You then need to read your essay and reread it. A key difference between good essays and bad is often the amount of time that you leave yourself to check and edit your work. A concise, well-presented essay will receive much better marks without you having to know more about the topic.

'Don't leave essays/seminar papers till the last minute – no matter how hideous the thought of them, they only get worse if left! Make a start on the reading asap and make notes as you go along. Do read and reread essays and seminars before you hand them in or present them.'

Deborah Hyde, first-year history student, Birkbeck College, University of London

Deadlines

Deadlines have to be met. You may have got into bad habits at school of handing work in late, but this is not generally tolerated at university. You can ask for an extension but only if you have a really good reason, which you couldn't have helped, like being ill. If this happens let your department know as soon as you can – contact the departmental secretary initially. You may be required to produce proof.

Passing exams

However your course is structured, you're unlikely to escape exams altogether. The important thing to remember about any exam is that you only need to pass – anything above that is a bonus. You won't be let into university if you're not capable of passing an exam so, providing you do enough work and give yourself time to revise, there's no need to panic.

'How well you do in an exam can be divided into one quarter how good you are at the subject, one quarter how hard you work, one quarter your exam technique and one quarter luck.'

Phil Agulnik, former University of London Union President

The usual rules about keeping healthy are even more important to follow when preparing for exams (see Chapter eight). Allow yourself time off, eat a healthy diet and get outside at least once a day. A study tested students' intellectual abilities before and immediately after they had taken aerobic exercise, and all showed marked improvement. So even if you've avoided exercise for the rest of the year think about spending time in the gym, jogging or cycling as exams get nearer. You can revert to being a couch potato the moment they are over.

Revision

Here are the golden rules of revision:

- leave plenty of time

- draw up a timetable that breaks your day down into chunks and build in some time off

- check with your tutors exactly what you need to revise

- organise your working space so that it's clear and free of clutter

- look at past papers – go to the library or ask your department

- gather all your notes together

- *start!*

'Start revising early, it may sound like it's a bit of a geeky thing to do but it's worth it! It prevents cramming at the end which, no matter what anyone says, doesn't work!'

Paul Blundell, first-year psychology student,
Lincoln University

Find out what topics you need to cover and collate your notes, books and essays into these topics. Allow plenty of time to do this. Swap essays with others on your course – this is a great way of covering additional information relatively painlessly. Do some timed essays. These are not only good revision aids but give you an idea of how much you can write in the time. Don't expect to reproduce everything you can in a term-time essay. Examiners know this is impossible and mark accordingly. For practical subjects make sure you have completed all your assessed projects and handed in your coursework on time.

'I've noticed that, in my course anyway, some people ask you to do work that is not worthwhile. It's better to look at past papers to know what's expected of you in exams.'

Jennifer Hogan, fourth-year natural sciences student,
Clare College, Cambridge University

Always condense the information each time you go over it, so you end up looking at less and less paper. Aim to end up with just a few facts that you commit to memory, which act as triggers to all you know about that topic.

Draw up a revision timetable that takes you up to your exams, and then break this down into daily timetables. Try to revise in chunks of about 45 minutes, and build in periods of relaxation and exercise. Most people find it easier to revise one topic at a time rather than jump around. Some people also find it helpful to revise with friends, although others find this intimidating.

Don't stay up the night before an exam. It might seem like the end of the world if you don't read that information just once more, but a tired brain acts in strange ways. You can end up squeezing out the information you've absorbed. Even if you've done very little work, you're better off sitting an exam with a refreshed brain. Exams are largely assessed on your response to the question, and a tired brain can't respond very effectively.

Finally, check when and where the exam is, how you are going to get there and how long it will take. If you have to travel to somewhere unfamiliar do a dummy run beforehand. Leave plenty of time – the last thing you need is to add to your exam stress by worrying about whether you are going to make it on time.

In the exam

Check what's required by reading the instructions – do this at least twice. If you have to carry out a project or experiment then double check your equipment to see if it's all there and working. Make sure your mobile is switched off!

Always answer all the questions you're supposed to. It is much easier to pass an exam by attempting to answer all questions, even those you're unsure of, than by trying to score exceptional marks for the questions you're confident of and leaving others out.

Technique is extremely important, follow the points listed below.

1. Read *all* the questions through carefully – read the whole paper before choosing the questions you answer.

2. Look at how many marks each question carries and work out how much time you have to spend – if one question carries 50% of the marks, spend 50% of your time on it.

3. Make a plan of your answer – this is never a waste of time.

4. Move on to the next question when your allocated time is up.

5. If your mind goes completely blank leave that question and continue with another one – you can always come back later once your confidence has returned. Don't waste time struggling.

6. Leave time to read your answers through – careless mistakes can slip through when you're writing at speed.

7. If you run out of time, write the information you planned to include in note form at the end of your answer – you may pick up the odd mark.

8. Write clearly and legibly. If the examiner can't read your writing they won't be able to follow your argument or calculations, and you may even have to pay to have your paper transcribed – it also won't endear you to your examiner.

If you have any specific needs, such as dyslexia, make sure you find out what additional provisions can be put in place for you.

Examiners aren't out to fail you. They award marks for every valid point you make, rather than knocking marks off for what you leave out. So use the examination time to prove to them what you know about your subject. Your tutors will warn you if they are seriously worried that you're going to fail.

Try to avoid comparing notes with others afterwards. It rarely makes you feel better, and it's now up to the examiners to judge how well you've done. Instead, try to focus on the next exam if you have one or go and do something you really enjoy doing to take your mind off things.

What happens if I fail?

If the worst happens and you fail a course then most departments will offer you a resit or allow you to retake a year. If there are reasons why you've failed your exams, other than not doing enough work, then let your tutors know as soon as possible. If there are medical reasons for you not doing well, then get a medical certificate from your doctor, preferably before you take the exam. Your students' union can provide further advice.

'In the first year I had some difficulties with some of my modules, but I talked to my head of department who helped me and I passed my resits. That's the only academic problem I have had.'

William Wilson, fourth-year management student, Aston University

---

Can I appeal?

Most universities allow you to appeal if you feel you've been unfairly treated in any aspect of your course and assessments. Get details from your students' union and tutors. Collect all the information you feel is relevant.

You can also be summoned to attend an academic appeal if your tutors or examiners feel you've been cheating or you have plagiarised someone else's work. These are formal affairs and you may be entitled to legal representation. Get advice immediately from your students' union.

Changing course

If you decide that you've chosen the wrong course then you can usually transfer quite easily providing you are not more than halfway through the second term of your first year, you want to transfer to another course within the same university, and that course isn't oversubscribed. Talk to your personal tutor as you'll need his or her help. Your tutor will also need to write to your local education authority. Changing modules can be a simple matter of filling out a registration form so that you are entered for the correct exam at the end. Changing courses during the first year of a degree course in Scotland is also straightforward.

However, if you want to transfer to another university or make the decision to change courses late, it can cause problems with your student loan and tuition fees and isn't nearly so straightforward. If this happens to you talk to your personal tutor and your students' union as you'll need advice.

> 'I changed from French and drama to Hispanic studies and politics at the end of my first year because I wasn't enjoying the course or being with the people on it. Because the transfer was within the same university this was relatively straightforward. I was lucky my university supported me as I was much happier with my second course and very glad that I changed.'
>
> **Anna Roberts, Hispanic studies and politics graduate, Queen Mary College, University of London**

Lifesavers

If you experience any academic difficulties speak to your course representative, your personal tutor or another lecturer with whom you get on. Or try your students' union, which can act as a mediator between you and the university.

Publications

There are loads of books offering advice on studying generally and for very specific subjects and courses. Here are a few general study guides to get you going.

How to Get a Good Degree (Open University Press, £15.99); *How to Pass Exams Every Time* (How To Books, £8.99); *Reading at University: A Guide for Students* (Open University Press, £15.99); *Student Friendly Guide: Sail Through Exams!* (Open University Press, £7.99); *Student Friendly Guide: Write Great Essays!* (Open University Press, £7.99) and *The Study Skills Handbook* (Palgrave Study Guides, £11.99).

Chapter four
Money

This chapter covers:

- Tuition fees – changes

- Money in

- Non LEA-funded courses

- Particular circumstances

- Making the pennies stretch

- Managing debt

- Serious problem?

- Lifesavers

Going to university is a hefty financial commitment these days. A MyEquifax/NUS survey found that the average student debt on graduation was £12,000, and 66% of students thought that it would take them between two and ten years to pay this off. And with the increase in tuition fees from 2006, student debt is likely to rise further.

You need to be clear about what you are entitled to, think about how you can maximise your income and be careful about how you manage your finances. If all this sounds a bit daunting then the good news is that learning these skills at university will equip you very well for the future – plus there are an awful lot of people in and around universities who can help steer you through.

'The main money problems I have had have always been as I reach the end of each term because the student loans come in at the beginning of each term, pretty much. Don't think that you have loads of money at the start of term because by the end of term those things that you bought when you thought you had loads of money will really annoy you!'

Elizabeth Hardaker, fourth-year biology masters student, University of Bath

Tuition fees – changes

In 2006, changes to student funding are being introduced. Universities in England will be able to charge students a contribution to their tuition fees of up to £3000 a year. However, students will be able to apply for a non means-tested student loan to cover this cost (i.e. the loan does not depend on your household income). This student loan will be on top of the maintenance loan you can take out to help cover your living costs. You only start paying both loans back once you are earning a certain amount each year, currently £15,000.

Universities planning to charge the maximum £3000 have had to sign up to an access agreement with the Office for Fair Access (www.offa. org.uk). (See *Additional university bursaries*, page 68.)

You don't have to pay fees for certain health professional courses (see *NHS-funded courses* page 76).

From 2006, students who normally live in Wales, regardless of where they study in the UK, will be able to apply for the student support package offered by the National Assembly for Wales. From 2006, Welsh students studying in England will be able to take out a loan of up to £3000 to cover the maximum tuition fees contribution English universities can ask for. Welsh students studying in Wales can take out a loan of £1200 to cover the maximum tuition fees contribution Welsh universities can ask for. Neither loan has to be paid back until after they graduate and start earning more than £15,000.

Northern Irish students are assessed in a similar way to English students, unless they live in Northern Ireland and study at a college in the Republic of Ireland, in which case the Irish Government will pay all tuition fees.

Scottish students who study at Scottish universities don't have to make any contribution towards their tuition fees, regardless of their family's income (although they have to pay a graduate endowment – see under *Scottish students* page 69). Scottish students studying at universities elsewhere in the UK will be assessed for contributions towards their tuition fees, as will students from other parts of the UK who study at Scottish universities.

Money in

It's vital that you make the most of the money available to you. For most students this comes from a combination of student loans, parental help, money they earn through part-time work and/or holiday work and bank overdrafts. However, even the most entrepreneurial of students will also have to be able to make the pennies stretch.

Student maintenance loans

Student maintenance loans are the main source of financial help available to students to help cover their living costs. They are the cheapest way of borrowing money.

Part of the student maintenance loan to cover your living costs is assessed on what your family earns. All eligible students can take out 75% of the student loan, but whether you can take out the other 25% will depend on your income or that of your parents, spouse or long-term partner. The amount of maintenance loan available is reduced by up to £1200 for those who qualify for a maintenance grant (see page 66). They recieve this money instead as part of their student maintenance grant, which they do not have to repay. This is intended to reduce the amount of debt for students from lower income backgrounds.

You have to apply for your student loan(s) each year (see *Applying for student loans,* page 7). **The Student Loans Company** (www.slc.co.uk) publishes the deadlines by which you must apply for student loans each year. The deadlines are different for new and existing students. Make sure you don't miss the deadline. The earlier you apply the better the chance that your loan will be paid at the beginning of each term.

Student loans are paid in three instalments – one at the beginning of each term.

Each year the maximum rate of student maintenance loan increases. In recent years these rises have matched inflation so that the amount the loan is worth stays the same. However, from 2006 the Government is going to raise the student maintenance loan by more than the rate of inflation. To find out how much the student loan is for the year you apply, visit the **Student Loans Company** website or one of the many students' finance websites listed in *Lifesavers*, page 89. You start repaying your loans once you finish your degree and start earning over £15,000, though this figure is reviewed annually. The repayments will include interest payments that are linked to the rate of inflation, so that what you pay back is worth the same as the amount that you borrowed.

'A good idea is to put your student loan into a savings account when you first get it, which is something I wish I had done.'

**Jeremy Carlton, PhD biochemistry student,
Bristol University**

The amount you pay back each month is linked to your earnings, so the more you earn, the more you repay. So someone earning £20,000 a year will have to repay £8.65 a week. If your income drops to below £15,000 then you stop making repayments. And if you don't earn £15,000 a year for 25 years after you graduate then the government writes the loan off.

The **Student Loans Company** and **HM Revenue and Customs** work together to collect payments. If you work for an employer then your loan repayments will be taken out of your salary through the Pay As You Earn (PAYE) scheme.

Maintenance grants

From 2006, a means-tested maintenance grant of up to £2700 a year (2006 rate) will be available to full-time students. Students from households with an annual income of £17,500 or less should get the full amount. Students whose families earn between £17,501 and £37,425 should be able to get a partial grant. In addition, universities must give students qualifying for the full grant a bursary that at least makes up the difference between the maintenance grant and the tuition fees they charge. So that if they charge £3000 a year in tuition fees then they must offer a student getting the full maintenance grant a bursary of at least £300 – many will offer more.

You need to apply to your **Local Education Authority (Education and Library Board** in Northern Ireland) at the same time as applying for your student loan(s). Grants are paid in three instalments – one at the beginning of each term. Maintenance grants and bursaries don't have to be paid back.

Who qualifies?

Residence: To qualify for financial support, you must have been 'ordinarily resident' in the UK for three years before the start of your course or have been granted 'settled status'.

From 2006, EU nationals who satisfy certain residency requirements can apply for maintenance loans and tuition fee loans in the same way as home students, providing you have lived in the UK for three years before the start of your course. If you are an EU national who doesn't live in the UK, then you are able to apply for a tuition fee loan but not a maintenance loan. For more information visit the **Department for Education and Skills (DfES)** website at www.dfes. gov.uk/studentsupport and follow the links for EU students.

Students from non-EU countries, commonly known as international students, have to pay the full cost of their tuition fees, although may be able to apply for a bursary or scholarship. It is vital that you make sure you have enough money to live and study in the UK before you leave your home country. You can find more information on the **British Council** website at www.educationuk.org or contact the British Council Office in your home country. You can also get information and advice from the **UK Council for International Education** (UKCOSA) – at www.ukcosa.org.uk

The course: You must also be attending a course that is eligible. The main ones are full-time first degree, Higher National, foundation degree and Diploma of Higher Education courses. If you are unsure, do check, as the Government is considering widening the number of courses that are eligible. The **Student Loans Company** at www.slc.co.uk has details.

N.B. If you have recieved financial support previously for higher education, you should check your entitlement with your local education authority.

Means-testing

As mentioned previously, part of the student maintenance loan for your living costs and all of the maintenance grant are means-tested. Whether you qualify and how much you get depends on your income and that of:

- your parents if you are not independent (see later)

- your spouse or long-term partner if you are over 25.

Your parents' income is not taken into account if you are judged to be an 'independent' student, that is:

- you are 25 or over by the time that you start your course

- you are married or have entered into a civil partnership

- you have been supporting yourself for three years before your course begins

- you are estranged from your parents, have been in care or have no living parents.

Additional university bursaries

Not all universities are planing to charge the maximum £3000 contribution towards tuition fees. Those universities that wish to charge the maximum have had to set up an access agreement with the Office for Fair Access (OFFA) to help offset the costs of tuition fees. These will take the form of non-repayable cash bursaries and scholarships to help support students from poorer backgrounds.

Most universities charging the maximum tuition fees contribution are offering more than the minimum £300 required by OFFA – many will be offering a bursary of around £1000 to those who qualify for the full maintenance grant. And many universities will also offer some bursary help to students whose family incomes fall just above the threshold for qualifying for the full maintenance grant.

However, the bursaries available vary from university to university and you should contact your individual institution for details of the schemes they run. There may be a great variety of support on offer, such as cash, scholarships, laptop computers and travel passes. Some will be means-tested according to your family income while others will be based on academic merit or only be available for certain courses.

Scottish students

Students living in Scotland before the start of their course and studying in Scotland are funded differently to the rest of the country. They can apply for:

- a student loan, which is partially means-tested

- a young person's bursary, if their family income is between £17,500 and £31,000

- an additional bursary

- help with travel costs to and from university, and with travelling from university to their family home.

You need to apply to the **Student Awards Agency for Scotland** who will carry out the assessment of your income and that of your family, make the award and administer its payment. Full contact details are in the *Lifesavers*, page 89, or visit www.saas.gov.uk

Scottish students who study at a Scottish university also have to pay a graduate endowment, currently just over £2000, when they graduate. This can either be paid as a lump sum or through a specially arranged student loan, which will then be repaid under the standard student loan system.

Welsh students

From 2006, responsibility for student support passes from the Department for Education and Skills to the National Assembly for Wales. This means that different rules can now operate in Wales and England.

Welsh students, regardless of where they study, can apply for the means-tested maintenance grant of up to £2700 to help with the cost of living expenses. Students with family incomes of up to £15,580 will be able to apply for the full grant with reduced grants being available to students from families with incomes of up to £32,774 (2006 figures). Grants do not have to be paid back.

Welsh students can also apply for the student loan that helps to cover living costs that is available to other UK students. Loans do have to be paid back. (See *Student maintenance loans*, page 65.)

Welsh students still have to apply through their Local Education Authorities to be assessed for the student support measures they are entitled to. Look on the internet under the name of your local council.

For more information visit the **Student Finance Wales** website at www.studentfinancewales.co.uk

Income from a job

Most students find they have to work while they are at university. If you need to work part-time during term time be careful – 30% of students who work during term time missed lectures because of their employment, according to a GMB/NUS survey. If you can afford to just work during the holidays then this is a better option.

'Get a job in the first and second years so that you don't have to work too much in the third year when you have less time.'

Vicky Spencer, third-year textile design student, Chelsea College of Art and Design

Some students' unions have a job shop or post details of part-time and holiday jobs. Check out **The National Association of Student Employment Services (NASES)** website, which has a job shop section, at www.nases.org.uk and don't forget the local papers and newsagents' windows. There's also more information on working part-time and during the holidays in Chapter five. Be careful that you don't end up paying too much tax and National Insurance (see *Student tax and NI*, page 96).

'Bills come at the worst possible times and you can do nothing but pay them. Probably my best advice would be to get a part-time job of some description, even if you're only earning £20 a week or so it makes all the difference.'

Peter Rodger, second-year biology student, Wentworth College, University of York

Parental contributions

Most students find that they have to rely on some money provided by their parents. It's best to agree with your folks what this is going to be before you go to university so that you can budget and your parents know what their commitments are. See *Making the pennies stretch*, page 81, for ideas about what your expenses are going to be.

It's obviously important to talk to your parents if you find that you are getting into money difficulties (see *Managing debt*, page 88) but try not to rely on them to bail you out all the time.

'I wouldn't have had enough money without my parents' help. Any problems I did have were mostly my fault – like wasting money on take-aways and eating out instead of cooking myself. You can usually just use your common sense to find out how to save money.'

Rob Lucas, third-year critical fine art practice student, Brighton University

If your parents aren't in a position to help you out, then find out about any money available from your university, sponsorship opportunities and grants.

Bank overdrafts

Most students end up using their bank overdrafts. This is why it is essential to check out which banks offer the best deal when choosing an account (see *Sorting out money*, page 18). If you need to you can usually arrange a bigger overdraft, but only do so when you have used up cheaper forms of debt, like your student loan. Additional overdrafts carry interest rates. Never go overdrawn without arranging an overdraft – the interest rates are much higher and you may well be charged administration fees on top. Phone up and be prepared to bargain, ideally having something to offer in return. This can be anything from a vacation job to your next loan instalment, providing it is not too far off.

Keep a record of how long your overdraft facility lasts, and don't automatically assume it will be continued after this date just because you don't have the money to pay it back. You'll have to renegotiate your facility.

'I had trouble getting an overdraft at the beginning. I hassled the bank and eventually managed to sort it out by phoning them and saying that I had no money, that most students were allowed an overdraft limit and just kept arguing until they gave it to me. I don't know why they caused difficulties.'

Rob Lucas, third-year critical fine art practice student, Brighton University

Banks take fees out of your account to cover various transactions such as bounced cheques, letters and interest on overdrafts. They are standard charges but can seem very steep when you have so little money. The best way to avoid bank charges is to arrange everything properly and keep records of all correspondence. Banks are often willing to waive charges if you explain your situation in advance.

Most banks will offer a student credit card, but be very careful about using it. The rates of interest will be far higher than your student loan or bank overdraft, about 17%, and there can be hefty penalties if you don't keep up with the payments. If you do take out a credit card then make sure you understand the terms and conditions, and be careful about how you use it.

Avoid store cards and catalogue credits. The rates of interest are high, it's difficult to keep track of when you have to pay off all the different accounts by (even if you do have the money) and the punishments for non-payment are swift and severe.

Access to Learning Fund

If you experience financial problems once you have started your course then your university may be able to help through the Access to Learning Fund. You need to be a full-time student, or a part-time student studying at least 50% of the equivalent full-time course.

The fund can help with things like:

- financial hardship

- emergency help for unexpected financial hardship

- costs that are not met by other grants.

Students are assessed according to their individual needs but generally priority is given to:

- students with children, especially lone parents

- other mature students, particularly those with existing financial commitments

- students from low income families

- disabled students

- students who have been in care

- students who are homeless

- students in their final year

- and students who are considering giving up their course because of financial hardship.

You need to apply directly to your university who will decide whether you are eligible. Payments are usually given as grants that don't have to be repaid but may also be given as short-term loans.

Don't struggle on in silence. If you are finding it difficult to manage financially then ask your university if it can help.

Sponsorship

Some companies sponsor students through university and pay them to work during the holidays. Science and engineering degrees are the ones most often sponsored. However, business and commerce-related subjects, such as economics and accountancy, can attract sponsorship. Sponsored students are often offered a job at the end of their degree too. You can also be sponsored through a 'student apprenticeship' scheme where you're employed by a company which offers you a combination of in-house training and higher education courses. Apply well in advance and be prepared to write to many companies before you find one that is interested in you.

'I did a 12-month placement in my third year. I had to find my own placement, apply and go for interview like for any job. I have to wait an extra year before I get my degree but personally I think it's good to have a year's work experience, it makes you more competitive in the job market. You can also pay off some of the debts you've made in the first two years!'

William Wilson, fourth-year management student,
Aston University

There can be disadvantages to being sponsored. Some companies require you to follow a particular course, so consider whether this is right for you without being swayed too much by the prospect of extra cash. And find out whether you'll be bound to the company after you've completed your course.

If you're a humanities student then sponsorship is probably not an option unless you have very strong contacts with a large company. But don't be afraid to ask. The worst that can happen is that they say no.

Some universities have sponsorship officers who can tell you more and help to find a company to sponsor you. If yours doesn't then you can find information about companies that sponsor students at your local Connexions/careers centre.

Look in libraries and Connexions/careers centres for an up-to-date copy of the *Educational Grants Directory* (Directory of Social Change).

Alternatively search online using the NUS Funding Finder at www.nusonline.co.uk

Forces sponsorship

The Army, Navy and Air Force offer sponsorship under two different schemes – bursaries and cadetships. Bursaries are given to students who don't want to commit themselves to a career in the forces immediately. Cadetships mean you join one of the Armed Forces and are paid a salary while at university. Under both schemes you have to attend training sessions at weekends, for which you'll be paid. The amount of time you have to serve in the force that has sponsored you varies according to whether you're awarded a cadetship or a bursary.

For more information see www.army.mod.uk; www.raf-careers.com and www.royal-navy.mod.uk

Scholarships

Some universities and professional institutions offer scholarships in certain subjects to particularly gifted students who may also have to fulfil other criteria such as academic background or residency requirements. Scholarships don't usually involve any work commitments, and they can be awarded in a variety of fields like sports, arts, music and science. Scholarships are usually oversubscribed and are likely to involve extra interviews and exams, though you won't have to pay them back. However, many more scholarships are likely to be available from 2006, as part of the extra financial help that universities will be offering to students. Ask your university about its scholarships, visit www.scholarship-search.org.uk or look in libraries and Connexions/careers services for a copy of *University Scholarships and Awards* (Trotman).

Charities

Some charities provide funds for courses, but you'll have to meet their very specific criteria. Some will only give funds to students who have already started a course and find they're not able to complete it because of a lack of money. If this is the case, you have to prove that you've explored all other avenues of funding.

The amount you get is likely to be limited and unlikely to fund an entire course, although it's possible to approach several organisations. Research the charity thoroughly so you can present your case well. For more information about charities with educational trusts look in libraries for the *Charities Digest,* the *Directory of Grant Making Trusts* and the *Educational Grants Directory.*

Non LEA-funded courses

Most undergraduate courses are funded by **Local Education Authorities, Education and Library Boards** and the **Student Awards Agency Scotland.** However, there are some exceptions to this and if it applies to your course you will have to apply for funding from the relevant organisation.

NHS-funded courses

A **National Health Service** bursary is a grant awarded to eligible students to cover everyday living costs such as accommodation. Further allowances may also be payable for:

- extra weeks' attendance

- older students

- initial expenses

- dependants

- single parents

- disabled students

- clinical placement costs.

Students who are in receipt of NHS bursaries will have their fees paid for them by the NHS. NHS bursaries do not have to be repaid.

Nursing and midwifery Diploma of Higher Education students are eligible for a non means-tested bursary (i.e. your household income is not assessed). If you receive a non means-tested bursary you can't apply for:

- student loans

- access or hardship funds

- the NHS hardship fund.

All other students on NHS-funded degree level programmes leading to professional registration (e.g. physiotherapist, speech and language therapist, radiographer, nursing degree course) are funded by a combination of means-tested bursaries (your household income is assessed) and reduced-rate student loans.

Once you are accepted on to an NHS-funded degree course then you will be contacted by the NHS Student Grants Unit covering the area where you live (see later). You also need to apply to your **Local Education Authority (LEA)** for your student support loan, which will be paid at a lower rate than students who are not funded by the NHS. The LEA will check your eligibility and let you know what your loan entitlement is.

Medical and dental students entering their fifth year of study (and any subsequent degree years) are eligible for a means-tested NHS bursary and a reduced-rate student loan and don't have to pay tuition fees.

A booklet titled *Financial Help for Healthcare Students* is available as a download from the Department of Health's website at www.doh.gov.uk (you need to do a general search or search the publications library).

For more information call NHS Careers on 0845 60 60 655.

Contact details:

- **NHS Student Grants Unit,** 22 Plymouth Road, Blackpool FY3 7JS (0845 358 6655)

- **NHS Wales Student Grants Unit,** 2nd Floor Golate House, 101 St Mary's Street, Cardiff CF10 1DX (029 2026 1495)

- **Student Awards Agency for Scotland (SAAS)** at Gyle View House, 3 Redheughs Rigg, South Gyle, Edinburgh EH12 9HH (0845 111 1711)

- **North Eastern Education and Library Board,** County Hall, 182 Galgorm Road, Ballymena, County Antrim BT42 1HN (028 2565 3333).

Teacher training

There are various financial incentive schemes available to students training to be teachers, such as the undergraduate Secondary Shortage Subject Scheme and the postgraduate tax-free bursary. You can find details on www.canteach.gov.uk or call the **Teacher Training Information Line** on 0845 6000 991 or for Welsh speakers on 0845 6000 992.

Social work

At the time of writing, students following approved degree-level social work courses can apply for an annual bursary and help with tuition fees (apart from in Scotland). More information and application packs are available from the **General Social Care Council** at www.gscc.org.uk

Dance and drama students

The Dance and Drama Awards scheme provides some students studying at private colleges taking part in the scheme with a contribution towards their tuition fees and help with their living costs. Call 0114 259 3612 for information. Other dance and drama colleges may offer their own scholarships. See also *Sponsorship,* page 74, *Charities,* page 75 and the Educational Grants Advisory Service in *Lifesavers,* page 89.

Particular circumstances

You may have particular circumstances or requirements that entitle you to additional funding for your university course.

Disabled students

If you have a disability or specific learning difficulty, like dyslexia, you may be able to claim for additional funds from your **Local Education Authority (LEA), Education and Library Board (ELB)** or the **Student Awards Agency for Scotland (SAAS).** Known as the disabled students' allowance, it is intended to meet the extra costs of studying that you incur because of your disability. It's not intended to meet the disability-related costs you have whether you study or not. Unlike tuition fee contributions and student loans it's not means-tested, so neither your nor your parents' or spouse's incomes will be taken into account.

'I have dyslexia and in my first year my university helped me apply to my LEA and I got a computer out of it!'

**Claire Baldwin, third-year history student,
Aberystwyth University**

You need to give your assessment authority medical proof of your disability from a doctor, audiologist, educational psychologist or specialist dyslexia teacher. If you haven't been assessed in the last two years then your LEA, ELB or the SAAS may need a new assessment, for which you may have to pay.

Some disabled students are able to claim income support, housing benefit and other benefits, to cover additional costs. You have to meet certain criteria to qualify for these benefits, so contact Skill or a local independent advice organisation such as the **Citizens Advice Bureau** (see *Lifesavers,* page 89) before you fill out any claim forms.

Skill: National Bureau for Students with Disabilities information service, 0800 328 5050; text phone, 0800 068 2422; website: www.skill.org.uk

An annual publication *Bridging the Gap: A Guide to the Disabled Students' Allowances in Higher Education* is available as a download from www.dfes.gov.uk/studentsupport/formsandguides/gui_guides.shtml

Students with dependants

Financial help is available for people who want to study and who have dependants.

- *Parent's Learning Allowance* of up to £1365 a year to help with course-related costs. How much you can get depends on your household income and does not have to be repaid.

- *Childcare Grant* for full-time students with dependant children in registered and approved childcare. The amount you can receive depends on your household income and your childcare costs. This help does not have to be repaid.

- *Adult Dependants' Grant* – if you have a husband, wife or partner or another adult family member who depends on you financially, you may be eligible for a grant. How much you can get depends on your household income and does not have to be repaid.

Guides with more information for students with children can be ordered from 0800 731 9133 and there is more information on the **Department for Education and Skills** website at www.dfes.gov.uk/studentsupport – you need to select 'students with children' from the left-hand menu.

Part-time students

Part-time students are not covered by the new Higher Education Act and so the fees that they are charged is not regulated. It is likely that part-time students will continue to have to pay their tuition fees up front and will not be eligible to take out a loan to cover the cost of their fees contribution.

However, there is some financial help available to part-time students who are studying at least 50% of the equivalent full-time course. They can apply for a non-repayable means-tested **fee grant** e.g. of up to a maximum of £750 for a course which is 50% of the full-time course and £1125 for a course which is at least 75% of a full-time course. They may also be able to get help with fees and other course costs through the Access to Learning Fund, which will increase in 2006 from £3 million to £12 million.

In addition, part-time students on low incomes can apply for a new non-repayable means-tested **course grant** of up to £250 a year to help with the cost of books, travel and course expenditure.

More information and developments in the support available to part-time students is available from the **Department for Education and Skills** information line on 0800 731 9133 or www.dfes.gov.uk/studentsupport – select part-time students from the left-hand menu.

Making the pennies stretch

You need to work out what you have to pay for and when you have to pay it. Paying certain things late can lead to real problems and be very difficult to sort out. Other things can be left though. You need to be able to prioritise. Don't be fooled by the relatively large sum of money deposited in your bank account at the beginning of term when you first receive your student loan. When you break this down into weekly amounts and realise that it has to last you for the whole term, and possibly the vacation, all of a sudden it seems very small.

As mentioned at the start of this chapter, a recent MyEquifax/NUS survey found that the average graduate debt is £12,000, and this can only rise after tuition fees rise from 2006. While this illustrates the point that you are going to have to watch your pennies, you are also more likely to earn more when you graduate. According to the *AGR Graduate Recruitment Survey 2005 (Winter Review)*, the average graduate starting salary is currently around £21,000, and your chances of standing in the job seekers' queue are reduced by 50%.

'The important thing is to work out a budget and keep to it. You need to include extras. I am living in a house which means that I don't just have rent but bills as well, which can be a lot to pay in one go.'

**Jonathan Clayton, third-year biochemistry student,
UMIST**

Budgeting is essential. The budgets here are based on the NUS budget 'What does it cost to be a student in 2005/2006' and the Aimhigher online 'cost of living' calculator. You can visit the NUS budget planner at www.nusonline.co.uk and the online 'cost of living' calculator at www.aimhigher.ac.uk The figures are based on two students in 2006/7 both living away from their parental home, one studying in London the other studying outside London. They both come from families with an annual household income of £33,000 so qualify for the maximum non means-tested part of the student maintenance loan, but don't receive a student maintenance grant.

	London	Outside London
Income		
Maintenance loan (the 75% that is available to all students*)	4627	3303
Income from work	210	160
Authorised bank overdraft	300	300
Total	**5137**	**3763**

* the extra 25% is means-tested, so you will receive it if your household income is below a certain level

Expenditure	London	Outside London
Course costs		
Other fees	14	14
Books, stationery, etc	325	136
Travel to university	641	452
Subtotal	980	602
Living costs		
Rent	3085	2215
Food, household goods	1764	1448
Household bills	813	813
Insurance	78	34
Phone/mobile	200	200
Travel (leisure)	657	582
Going out/leisure	1486	1486
Clothes	455	455
Subtotal	8538	7233
Total expenditure	**9518**	**7835**
Shortfall	**4381**	**4072**

The first seven items on the expenditure list (i.e. all of your course costs and down to insurance on your living costs) are the things that you should prioritise – they are known as your essential expenditure. Work out what they cost. Some people find it helps to set up a separate bank account for their essential expenditure. Work out how much you have left for non-essentials. Divide whatever this turns out to be into weekly amounts and only take this amount of money out of the cashpoint each week.

'My main difficulties were with money, every student finds that. You realise how much everything costs – you have to pay for food, books, clothes, social life. It's hard to strike a balance, especially in the first year when you suddenly have the freedom to go out every night of the week. You have to weigh up your priorities.'

Samantha Northey, third-year Chinese student, Edinburgh University

Rent

Rent is the largest sum of money you have to find from your funds and it must be a priority. If you live in a hall of residence then pay your fees as soon as you get your loan and any grants. If you pay your rent right at the start then you won't have to worry about it again.

If you live in a privately-rented house consider setting up a separate bank account for rent and bills. You can transfer the proportion of your loan you need to cover this, and not have to worry about finding the rent each month.

Food

Save money by:

- writing a weekly menu and buying only the ingredients you need

- keeping your eyes open for 'multi-buy' or special offers

- buying in bulk and cooking in bulk, although you need to store food properly

- shopping late at night, especially on a Sunday, as many stores reduce prices dramatically on goods approaching their sell-by dates

- visiting markets just before the stallholders are about to go home

- buying things in season – they are cheaper and fresher

- buying loose vegetables and fruit rather than the ones already packaged

- avoiding buying prepared and processed food – it's much more expensive and you can prepare your own, more nutritious meals in the same time (see *Healthy eating*, page 153).

'Economy shopping is the main way to save money. Compare prices in the area and buy from the cheapest. Also, keep an eye out for bargains – 'buy-one-get-one-free' offers are really good for saving a lot of money.'

Allan Jones, third-year geography student, Lancaster University

Household bills

Save money by:

- signing up to the companies that offer the best deals in your area – check out www.uswitch.com or www.saveonyourbills.com for information
- letting the council know you are a student so you don't have to pay Council Tax
- paying your TV licence on time – it can be done each month by direct debit
- reading meters and checking that you are being billed for the right amount
- turning things off when you aren't using them
- having a timer on your boiler so that the central heating and hot water are only on at times when you need them
- only boiling as much water in the kettle as you need
- wearing extra layers.

'Simple things can help, like remembering to turn the lights off when you leave a room and putting an extra jumper on instead of turning on the heating. It's all a question of making the effort.'

Allan Jones, third-year geography student, Lancaster University

Phones/mobiles

Save money by:

- signing up to the company that offers the best deal – check out www.uswitch.com or www.saveonyourbills.com for information

- changing your mobile to 'pay as you go' as it's much easier to keep track of costs

- signing up for deals that give you cheap national and international calls

- knowing when it's cheaper to use your phone/mobile

- keeping a clock by the phone so you can check how long you've been chatting.

'Take care with mobile phone bills as they can be huge unless you are very careful (as I've found to my cost) and hide your credit card as soon as you receive it.'

Peter Rodger, second-year biology student, Wentworth College, University of York

Travel

Save money by:

- travelling at off-peak times whenever possible

- cycling and walking as much as possible

- buying monthly travel cards

- always asking if there are any discounts for students

- planning well so you aren't making unnecessary journeys.

'Travelling is the main problem. It costs £50 a week to go by train because I live at home and I have to be in by 10am, so I pay the peak travel rate.'

Vicky Spencer, third-year textile design student, Chelsea College of Art and Design

Insurance

Even when money is tight it's still sensible to have some basic insurance for your belongings (see *Insurance*, page 18). But don't be tempted by extended warranties when buying anything new, however persuasive the sales person is – as these are rarely good value for money.

Going out/leisure

Save money by:

- not going out more than you can afford

- thinking of cheaper 'alternatives' such as hanging out at a mate's house

- working out how much you can spend in one evening and only taking that amount out of the cashpoint

- not getting suckered into buying endless rounds for people who never put their own hands in their pockets

- drinking slowly

- sussing out the area and sticking to the cheaper pubs and clubs

- having a coffee at home rather than buying one from the coffee shop

- taking a packed lunch and snacks out with you

- not being tempted to 'treat' yourself.

'If you only take out the amount of money that you want to spend each week, then you won't overspend. Also, when you go on a night out, don't take a credit or cash card with you, only the cash you want to spend.'

**Jeremy Carlton, PhD biochemistry student,
Bristol University**

Books

Save money by:

- not buying all the books on your reading list – see which books are essential to buy and which you can get from the library

- buying books from former students or second-hand book shops – many universities also have regular book sales

- getting to know www.swotbooks.com the website run by academic booksellers offering academic books at around 40% of bookshop price

- selling your textbooks once you've finished with them

- using NUS and student discounts.

Stationery

Save money by:

- buying all your stationery from students' union shops

- keeping your eyes open for commercial stationers offering student discounts

- using as much free stationery provided by the university as you can.

Clothes

Save money by:

- asking relatives to buy the expensive items you want

- rummaging around markets, second-hand shops and sales for bargains

- shopping in places like Primark, TK Maxx, H&M and New Look

- getting shoes and boots mended

- making your own clothes

- accessorising to change your look.

Managing debt

However careful you are, you may find that there are times when the money isn't there. Don't panic. Debt is part of student life.

First go over what you are spending and think about whether you can reduce your expenditure. Your rent, food and travel are all vital, but remember if you don't pay the bills of the utility companies they'll cut you off and you'll be landed with an extra reconnection charge. Make sure you have claimed all the money that you can. If things still don't add up then get some advice from your students' union, your university advice centre or one of the organisations listed in *Lifesavers*, page 89.

Serious problem?

If you find that some or all of the points below strike a chord, then you might be in serious debt and should get help immediately. Debts don't go away if they are ignored – they get worse.

- You are worried about your debts and feel stressed.

- You are leaving bills unopened.

- You are receiving letters saying that you owe money.

- You are using a credit card to pay for everyday things like food, because you can't pay any other way.

- You are only paying off the bare monthly minimum on credit and store cards.

- You are borrowing money from friends without being able to pay it back.

- Utilities and/or your phone has been cut off.

- Your university is withholding your degree or asking you to leave because you owe money.

- Bailiffs are knocking on your door.

If you have experience of the last three points on this list then you are likely to be in serious trouble. This doesn't mean that things can't be sorted out. Most organisations are willing to make payment arrangements with you, as this is much cheaper than taking court action against you. However, you are likely to need some help to get things sorted out. Your students' union, the university advice centre, the local **Citizens Advice Bureau** or a debt counselling service will all be able to advise.

Whatever you do, don't take out an unsecured loan. It's easy to get these loans, but the rates of interest are crippling and you'll end up in even greater debt.

Lifesavers

- English and Welsh students should contact their **Local Education Authority** (listed on the internet under the name of your local council) for an assessment of the money that they are entitled to.

- There's also lots of information on the **Department for Education and Skills** website, including application forms you can download, at www.dfes.gov.uk/studentsupport

- Welsh students can find information at the website run by the **National Assembly for Wales** at www.studentfinancewales. co.uk

- Students living in Northern Ireland need to apply to their local **Education and Library Board** for an assessment of their personal entitlement to support. General information and contact details for ELBs are available from the **Department for Employment and Learning** website at www.delni.gov.uk

- Scottish students can get more information and apply for a personal assessment of the support they are entitled to from **Student Awards Agency for Scotland** at www.student-support-saas.gov.uk

- For information about student loans contact **Student Loans Company**, 100 Bothwell Street, Glasgow G2 7JD. Tel: 0800 405 010; text phone, 0800 085 3950; website, www.slc.co.uk

Money advice

If you are not eligible for Government support, if you have exhausted all other forms of funding or if you are thinking about going to university and want advice on the support you might be entitled to, then send a large stamped addressed envelope to: **Educational Grants Advisory Service,** 501–505 Kingsland Road, London E8 4AU. Tel: 020 7254 6251; website: www.egas-online.org

For advice on money management, debt and dealing with people you owe money to, visit your nearest Citizens Advice Bureau. Details of local branches and online advice available from **National Association of Citizens Advice Bureau** at www.nacab.org.uk

For telephone counselling on all aspects of debt and financial management ring the **National Debtline** on 0808 808 4000 between 10am and 4pm Monday and Thursday, 10am to 7pm Tuesday and Wednesday, and 10am to noon on Fridays (www.nationaldebtline. co.uk).

Alternatively, you can call the **Consumer Credit Counselling Service Student Debtline** on 0800 328 1813 (www.cccs.co.uk).

You can also get online advice from **Credit Action** at www. creditaction.org.uk

Publications

Balancing Your Books: The CRAC Guide to Student Finance (available through Trotman, £6.99); *Students' Money Matters* (published annually by Trotman, £14.99) and *Student Survival: The Push Guide to Money* (published annually by Nelson Thornes, £9.95).

Chapter five
Jobs

This chapter covers:

- Part-time jobs
- Holiday work
- Work placements
- Volunteering
- Getting paid
- Student tax and National Insurance
- Impressive CVs
- Covering letters
- Application forms
- Psychometric tests
- Researching a company
- Interviews
- Lifesavers

Increasingly, students have to take on paid work in order to make ends meet. Figures from the Department for Education and Skills show 58% of students now work during term time. The UNITE Student Living Report 2004 found that the largest group (33%) work in the retail industry, with 28% pulling pints, waiting tables or working in kitchens. The remainder find jobs in offices, their university, call centres, or as care workers etc.

Part-time jobs

A 2004 survey found that, on average, students worked 14 hours a week, but many students felt that working part time while studying was one of the worst aspects of university life. The **Association of Graduate Careers Advisory Services (AGCAS)** recommends that you don't work more than 15 hours a week. Most major studies have shown that working more than this means your course suffers. If you need to earn more money, try combining working part time during term time with working in the holidays. Use the budget in *Making the pennies stretch*, page 81, to help you work out exactly how much you need to earn from a job.

Start by looking for part-time jobs in and around the university. Many universities employ students and have jobs websites and noticeboards. Ask at your students' union for details. The range of work available varies, but generally you can find bar work, shop work and stewarding at events on campus, although there may be a waiting list. Some universities also pay students for things like photography commissions, market research, proofreading or helping to run careers fairs.

Local part-time job opportunities will be listed in local newspapers, shop windows, etc. It's also worth just asking shops, bars, etc. whether they have any vacancies – particularly if you have a favourite place where you'd like to work. Go armed with a CV (see page 98) that you can leave with them. In addition, check out the Jobcentre Plus site at www.jobcentreplus.gov.uk and the graduate jobs websites (see page 214) some of which carry details of part-time and vacation work.

While your main motivation for getting a part-time job might well be financial it's also worth taking a step back and considering what your part-time job offers you in terms of CV building skills. Although working in a supermarket or local bar may not be your ideal occupation, you will be learning valuable lessons about dealing with people, handling money, managing difficult situations and being disciplined and organised. Don't think that employers won't be impressed by these skills. Of course, you may be lucky enough to land a job that gives you a foot in the door of your chosen career, like answering the phones at a local radio station or doing administrative shifts at a solicitors' office.

'I don't think I will use my degree when I graduate. I remember reading in the prospectus before I started my course that most geographers don't use geography in their chosen career but become accountants or something! I'm not saying that's what I will do, but my choice of career won't depend on what I studied at university.'

**Allan Jones, third-year geography student,
Lancaster University**

Holiday work

Holiday work can offer some more interesting and lucrative opportunities than part-time working during term time, but it can depend on where you stay in the holidays. Obviously, there will be more job opportunities in your large university town than your parents' sleepy village, but having to pay for accommodation will eat into your profits. Start by doing your sums.

Look for work in Jobcentre Plus offices and high street job agencies. And look out for seasonal opportunities. The Post Office, for example, employs extra workers during the Christmas holidays and there'll be seasonal harvesting and fruit-picking opportunities in rural areas. Leisure industries, such as hotels, catering outlets, arts festivals and sports centres also need extra pairs of hands at times when students are on holiday. Try sending off your CV (see page 98) to places you'd be interested in working in, calling them up and knocking on doors. There are lots of ideas, together with a directory of vacancies, listed in *Summer Jobs in Britain* (Vacation Work Publications, £10.99).

'Ribena is made by students. I started off shoving blackcurrants into the mill and after a couple of summers I became a skilled machine operator. This meant pushing a few buttons once in a while. I got through 14 novels that summer. I can't touch anything with blackcurrants in, but it was a good way of making some money and new friends.'

Chris Evans, history graduate, University of London

You can also work during the holidays while travelling abroad. While this sort of work is unlikely to earn you enough to bring a smile to your bank manager's face, it can be a good way of funding trips abroad while building up some useful skills for your CV (see *Working abroad*, page 98).

Work placements

Work placements are short-term work opportunities that give you a real taster of what it is like to work for a particular company. You will be paid a wage while you are there, and usually get the chance to carry out a specific project. Doing a sandwich degree or being sponsored by a company will mean that you have to complete a work placement as part of your degree (see *Sponsorship*, page 74).

Work experience is similar to doing a work placement, apart from you may not be paid a salary. Most companies will pay your travel expenses and you may sometimes get a lunch allowance or vouchers, too. However, work experience gives you very valuable hands-on experience and the opportunity to try out something before making any commitments.

'I was interested in finding out more about working in television so I looked up the websites of the main TV channels and production companies and sent a CV and covering letter to the addresses they gave. I was in a small department but learned a lot of things I had no idea about before and I enjoyed myself. If you are interested in something, go for it – even if you think you don't stand a chance.'

Isabelle Brewerton, fourth-year modern and medieval languages student, Corpus Christi College, Cambridge University

---

To organise a work placement or work experience write to companies you are interested in and ask them whether they run any schemes (see *Impressive CVs*, page 98 and *Covering letters*, page 100). Follow this up with a phone call or two, but don't harass them! Be prepared to make several enquiries before you find an opportunity. Some companies carry information about schemes on their websites, so do your research first (see also *Researching a company*, page 102).

There's more information, and work placements are listed on www.work-experience.org together with details of the free annual magazine *Focus on Work Experience*.

If you get work experience or a placement then make the most of it by:

- turning up on time, smartly dressed

- being friendly and asking how you can help

- being sensitive to people's work pressures

- going to lunch with your colleagues if you are offered the chance

- asking people how they got into the industry and what advice they would give

- doing the work you are given diligently, checking carefully for any errors

- asking someone in the office to write a short open reference for you.

If you enjoy the experience then ask whether they have any graduate entry schemes and make sure you leave a copy of your CV (see *Impressive CVs*, page 98) with the personnel or HR department. It might be worth staying in touch with the people that you have worked with by dropping the occasional email to remind them who you are (some companies have a high turnover of work experience people) and that you would be interested in working for the company. But don't bombard them!

Volunteering

Three in ten students do some sort of voluntary work while they are in university, according to the UNITE Student Living Report 2005, and six in ten give money to charities. Spending some time volunteering gives you fantastic experience and is great for your CV. The range of jobs you can get involved in is huge, from helping out at events to working with children, from working in a shop to helping raise funds. It won't help pay the bills but the rewards you get personally will be enormous, and it will definitely help you stand out from the crowd when you come to apply for your first graduate job.

'I got involved in societies focusing and campaigning on development issues, poverty and human rights. This kind of experience is really useful – both in terms of finding a job and in finding out about what kind of work you want to do.'

Amy North, MSc development studies student, London School of Economics, University of London

---

Your university may offer volunteering opportunities through the societies that it runs, or through things like **Student Community Action and Rag.** (See *Students' unions*, page 33.) To find details of your nearest student volunteering group visit the **Student Volunteer England** website at www.studentvol.org.uk There are also volunteering opportunities in the UK and overseas listed at www.do-it.org.uk

Getting paid

The national minimum wage applies to students as well as other workers and you should make sure that you are paid it. It is there to make sure that you are paid fairly for your time. From October 2005, the national minimum wage is:

- £5.05 an hour for people aged 22 and over (rising to £5.35 in October 2006 – subject to confirmation)

- £4.25 an hour for people aged 18 to 21 (rising to £4.45 in October 2006).

Student tax and National Insurance

Your employer takes your tax and National Insurance out of your wages directly through the Pay As You Earn (PAYE) scheme. However, there's a certain amount that you can earn each year before you have to pay tax, known as the personal allowance. In 2005/2006 this is £4895. Over this you normally pay:

- 10% on anything you earn between £4895 and £6985

- 22% on anything above this (up to £32,400)

- 40% on anything above £32,400.

You also have National Insurance deducted from your wages, currently at a flat rate of 11%, but it doesn't start until you earn at least £94 a week. Many students are exempt from paying National Insurance – check your wage slips to make sure you aren't being charged unnecessarily.

You are able to earn up to the maximum personal allowance for each tax year (April to April). This means that if you only work during the holidays and don't expect to earn more than the personal allowance for that tax year you can ask your employer for Form P38(S). Fill this in and you won't have any tax taken out of your wages.

However, if you already have a part-time job during term time, you won't be able to use this form just for your holiday job. You will already be 'on the system'. Unfortunately, this frequently means that students end up paying too much tax. Without a form to say that you are unlikely to earn more than the minimum wage during the course of the year, employers have to put you on an emergency tax code which takes off 22% tax and 11% National Insurance. You can claim this back at the end of the year using the Repayment Claim Form P50. It can be a bit time consuming but is well worth doing as you can get up to a third of your wages back.

There is an online tax checker on the HM Revenue and Customs website at www.hmrc.gov.uk/students that you can use to check if you are paying too much tax. You can also use this site to find out about claiming tax back.

When you leave a job, you will be given Form P45. Keep this safe and give it to your next employer, as it can help make sure you don't pay too much tax in your next job.

Working abroad

If you work abroad, then you have to pay the same taxes that you would if you were working in this country and the same personal allowances apply. If your overseas employer taxes you as well then you have to claim it back when you return to the UK.

If you are already working then you must fill in Form P85 and send it to the tax office to tell them you are going overseas.

You can find more information, as well as details of your nearest tax office, from the HM Revenue and Customs website at www.hmrc. gov.uk/students

Sandwich students

If you are a sandwich student you can qualify for certain tax free payments to cover your living costs while you study. These exemptions do not cover any money you earn while you are working for the employer, say in the holidays. Ask your employer whether they have any such schemes. You can also find more information at www.hmrc. gov.uk/students

Impressive CVs

Your CV is your introduction to future employers and people who you want to do work experience with. It needs to create a good impression.

Although you'll always hear tales of people lying on their CVs and getting away with it, generally, it is a really bad idea. With the internet and databases it is much easier to check facts, and you never know how diligent your prospective employers will be in following things up or who they know.

It's much better to stick to the facts but present your experience, even if it is limited, in a positive way which emphasises your skills. Try to use 'active' words like 'organised' and 'achieved', but avoid using too many 'I did this' phrases. A few can be useful, but too many get in the way of the information. And keep information short and to the point – you don't want to bore the recruiter before they get to the end.

Joe King
07770 123456
joeking@universitycollegecampus.ac.uk

Holiday contact: 12 Crown Street, London SW2 2ZZ 020 7123 4567
Term-time contact: Room 22, Building 2, University College Campus, Regent Street, Coventry CV2 2ZZ 024 1234 5678

Personal profile

An enthusiastic finalist with good research and writing skills, a confident communicator and keen team player.

Education

2003 to present: University College, Coventry – English and Media Studies (predicted result 2.1) Modules include twentieth-century English, the development of script to screen, and practical units in camera operation and editing. Requires regular group presentations and producing practical work to deadlines.

1996–2003: Scholar School, London – Three A levels: English (A), drama (B) and French (B). Awarded the sixth-form prize for English and was leader of the orchestra.

10 GCSEs with four subjects at A* and two at A, including English Language and maths.

Work experience

February 2004 to present: University bar tender
A member of the term-time bar staff team responsible for keeping the bar running smoothly even when busy, balancing the tills and dealing face to face with customers. Includes training in stock taking and ordering.

June–August 2004: Local newspaper – London
Two-month work placement in a busy newsroom conducting interviews, researching copy for articles and assisting in running the office, including coordinating the section editor's diary.

December 2003: Post Office – London
Relief postal worker responsible for sorting mail. Required attention to detail and good organisational skills.

2001–2002: Deep Kleen Kleeners – London
Saturday shop assistant at local dry cleaning business, responsible for dealing with customers, balancing the tills and organising the shop.

Skills

- Excellent research and writing skills honed through practical journalistic experience.
- Confident communicator used to dealing with people face to face and on the phone in a great variety of circumstances.
- Computer literate in most word processing and email packages, plus Excel and Photoshop.
- Increasing familiarity with video editing software.

Interests

- I follow my interest in journalism by regularly writing for my student newspaper, mainly for the news section.
- I play the violin to Grade 8 standard and have joined the university orchestra.
- I enjoy travelling and spent a month touring round Greece in 2003.

References available on request

How you organise your CV depends a bit on the experience that you have had. People with a lot of experience may want to organise their CVs according to their key skills, but unless you are confident about that format it's best to stick to something more traditional, like the one shown.

Make sure that your CV is clearly typed in at least 11 point font, is free from fancy typefaces, doesn't run to more than two sides of A4 and is clearly printed on good quality paper. You should also avoid too much elaborate formatting, particularly if you need to email your CV. If you have to send it through the post then use a hard-backed envelope, so that it doesn't arrive dog-eared.

You don't have to include your age, marital status or state of health – it is illegal for employers to discriminate against you on these grounds. Nor should you write 'Curriculum Vitae' across the top of the page. It will be obvious what it is from the layout and you want people to remember the most important detail – your name – so make sure it is at the top.

And finally, check, check and check again. Your CV needs to be 100% accurate. Get a friend to help you, as it's really difficult to spot your own mistakes, then show it to an expert – a careers adviser. Your university should have one. If not, look on the internet for details of your nearest one. Connexions/careers services may also be able to help.

'There is a great careers service in Edinburgh – you can go and talk to an adviser and they are really helpful. They take you through your CV and if you have any questions they show you where to look and who to contact.'

Samantha Northey, third-year Chinese student, Edinburgh University

---

Covering letters

No CV, however wonderful, should be sent off without a covering letter. A covering letter introduces you and lets the employer know how you heard about them. It should fit easily onto one side of A4 and run to around four paragraphs. In the first paragraph state where you saw the job advertised and the title of the job you are applying for, if you are responding to an advertisement. If you are requesting work experience then use the first paragraph to say, briefly, how you know about the company and why you are interested in it.

In the second paragraph elaborate on the skills you can offer them, but be careful of just repeating your CV. Instead, focus on specific skills your course or interests have given you and why you think they apply to the job or company.

Then reiterate your interest in the position or company. Finally, sign off with a positive phrase which anticipates them wanting to see you, such as 'I look forward to hearing from you.' Your covering letter should be typed, unless a company specifically requests a hand-written letter, and in the same typeface and font as your CV.

'After I'd researched the companies I was interested in on the internet I then sent my CV and covering letter to the ones I thought sounded interesting. I think it is really important that you use your covering letter to really explain your interests and experience – otherwise you could end up just being overlooked.'

Amy North, MSc development studies student, London School of Economics, University of London

---

Application forms

Some companies produce job descriptions and person specifications and require you to apply using an application form. The key to filling out a successful application form is sticking to the point. Read the job description and person specification carefully, then make sure that each answer you give on the application form relates to one of the points in the person specification, wherever possible. If you come across a question where your experience doesn't quite fit with the person specification try to make a close match or say that this is an area you are interested in developing. Make sure that you answer every single question asked – even if you write n/a (not applicable) against an answer. This is so that the potential employer knows that you have not just left it out or not spotted it.

Psychometric tests

Some companies use psychometric tests, which are questionnaires designed to reveal your personality, motivations and career ambitions. The nature of these tests means that companies are looking for 'right' and 'wrong' answers and the best way of preparing for them is to get some practice. You can find examples by putting 'psychometric tests' into an internet search engine or by visiting www.shldirect.com There are also a number of books on the market, such as *How to Master Psychometric Tests* (Kogan Page, £8.99).

Psychometric tests tend to be broken up into three papers – verbal skills, mathematical ability and personality tests. The verbal papers are like language comprehension tests and the more you do the more familiar you will become with the style. Respond to each question by asking yourself, 'Does my answer follow on logically from the information that I have been provided with?' If your maths is a bit dodgy then make sure you swot up on things like percentages, ratios, basic statistics and graphs. And when it comes to the personality tests just be yourself. Don't try to second-guess the answers that the company is looking for – you could end up skewing your personality in the wrong direction!

Make sure that you read the instructions carefully and then get on with providing your answers. Don't waste time by spending ages agonising over the 'right' answer. With ability tests you are likely to score higher marks the more questions you get through, so make a decision and move on. You also need a clear head to score highly in psychometric tests, so avoid drinking alcohol the night before and make sure you get a good night's sleep. Eat a good, filling breakfast and arrive in plenty of time.

Researching a company

'I would definitely recommend looking up information about the company that is interviewing you – what they do, what you would be expected to do. I had a really embarrassing interview when I didn't know anything about the company!'

Amanda Warburton, microbiology with medical bioscience graduate, Kent University

Avoid looking like a fool by doing some thorough research on the company – preferably before applying for a job, but certainly before you attend an interview. It's a bit like revising for one of your exams. If you know the history of the company, what it does and what its plans are then you won't get any surprise questions.

The internet is a blessing. Most companies have websites, so visit them and read the information thoroughly. Do an internet search to find out if the company has been in the news recently and why. Pick up trade journals from libraries or university careers services to get an idea of the industry in general and to check for recent mentions of the company.

Some universities run schemes where you can speak to graduates of your university who now work in that company. If your university has this scheme then use it. There's nothing like a personal chat to get you clued up and to give you a true picture of what working for that company is really like. Websites are very useful but they will only give you the 'official' line. And if you get the chance to mention to the interviewers that you have done this you will score big initiative points!

Don't despair if your university doesn't have such a scheme. Try family, friends, parents of friends, their relatives, their friends – you never know who might know someone who is working in that company. Spread the word and see what happens.

'I would say that the best thing you can do in a job interview is to be yourself. I knew about the job that I was applying for and prepared by reading up on the company and the profession.'

Sarah Brown, maths graduate, Christ's College, Cambridge University

Interviews

Psychologists estimate that it takes a fraction of a second for someone to make a judgement about you, so it is very important to create a good first impression. If you create a bad impression you have to create five or six good impressions before someone will think differently about you – that's a lot of hard work when you want to be concentrating on answering the questions asked. So dress smartly. Your student loan may not stretch to a suit, but try to buy or borrow a jacket and wear it with smart trousers or a skirt. Make sure that your hair is freshly washed and neat. Avoid carrying any big bags and definitely don't bring your shopping to an interview. It will be difficult to create a good impression if you are struggling in through the door and then searching for somewhere to put everything. If you want or need to take examples of your work then buy or borrow a folder or portfolio case.

Plan your route. It may sound over the top, but if you don't know the area where the company is then it is as well to do a 'dummy' run so that you are confident about where you are going and how long the journey will take. Allow plenty of time to get there and take maps with you even if you are fairly sure you know where to find the company. You don't want to add to your pre-interview nerves by fretting about whether you are going to get there on time, and if you're in a panic it's easy to get lost. Sometimes companies send a map out with the interview confirmation letter, but take an A–Z as well as these maps are sometimes not very detailed or are awkward to read. And take the confirmation letter with you too. It will tell you where to go, what time you have to be there, and if the receptionist looks blankly at you when you arrive, you'll have your evidence to hand.

'It's a really good idea to plan things like your transport, clothes and so on in advance so that you can be calm and focused on the day.'

Sarah Brown, maths graduate, Christ's College, Cambridge University

Arrive at your interview no later than five minutes before it is due to start – but don't arrive too early either. Arriving very early can annoy people who have scheduled you an appointment time, may well be in the middle of interviewing another candidate and don't want to take a call from reception telling them you are here 30 minutes before you are due.

Find out who will be interviewing you in advance and what their position in the company is. If this information isn't in the confirmation letter then ring. It means you won't look blank when you meet them face to face or be distracted by trying to remember who they are and what they do, instead of concentrating on your answers. You may be interviewed by two or even three people. When you are introduced to them, look them confidently in the eye and give a good firm handshake – this all communicates confidence even if you are shaking in your boots. Be careful not to stare them out or crush their bones though. Smile and say how nice it is to meet them and thank them for seeing you, then sit in the seat indicated and prepare to face their questions.

The more research you have done (see *Researching a company*, page 102) and the better you have prepared, the stronger chance you will stand. Look back over your application and the details of the job you were sent, think about the questions they might ask and prepare some answers.

'It is really important to have worked out why you want to do that kind of job and why you would be good at it. Be positive and flag up all the relevant experience you have.'

Amy North, MSc development studies student, London School of Economics, University of London

Some standard interview questions are listed below.

- Describe your experience so far.

- Why do you think you are a good candidate?

- What attracts you to this post?

- What do you think are the key responsibilities of this job and how do they relate to your experience?

- Why should we give this job to you when we have more experienced candidates applying?

- Where do you see yourself in five years' time?

- Do you prefer working as part of a team or taking on your own projects?

- Would you be prepared to work some weekends and evenings?

- What are your strengths and weaknesses?

You may also be asked a 'role play' question where you are presented with a situation you are likely to encounter in the job, such as a tight deadline or apparently conflicting priorities. What interviewers are looking for here is a logical approach to that situation, which demonstrates your understanding of prioritising. There's unlikely to be a 'right' answer – they will be more interested in seeing how you think.

Try to answer each question clearly without rambling, drawing on relevant practical examples to illustrate your skills. Don't forget that your degree will have equipped you with research, writing, presentation and public speaking skills, all of which are invaluable to employers whatever job you are applying for – you can use examples from it too. Don't be afraid of a pause, these are natural in conversation and can allow time for you to gather your thoughts. And do ask for a question to be repeated or rephrased if you don't quite understand it, rather than blunder in and try to bluff your way through. Finally, if you really get stumped and don't know the answer it's much better to admit that than lie or stumble over an answer. The question may have been a trick one anyway!

Have some questions lined up at the end of the interview as it demonstrates an interest in the company. Here are some suggestions.

- Are there any training opportunities attached to this position?

- Typically, what have people in this post gone on to achieve?

- How much contact does this department have with other departments?

- Is the role mainly office-based or are there opportunities to meet clients?

- How will you be letting candidates know of your decision?

'Prepare questions to ask them in advance so that when they say 'Do you have any questions?' you don't have an embarrassed silence, and it shows that you are interested.'

Amanda Warburton, microbiology with medical bioscience graduate, Kent University

Interviews can seem daunting but the key thing to remember is that you are there because you have presented an application that meets their criteria and interests them. They are interested in what you have to say. So try to relax, remember to smile and present the best case you can.

At the end, stand up and shake hands and smile. Thank them for seeing you and say that you look forward to hearing from them soon. Then go out and do something that you really enjoy, like meeting friends, seeing a film or playing a sport to take your mind off the interview. There's nothing else you can do now – the decision is in their hands.

Lifesavers

Make the most of your university Careers Advice Service for help with job finding, CV writing, job application, interview techniques and careers advice.

There are also several publications you might find helpful: *CVs and Applications* (Lifetime Careers Publishing, £10.99); *Jobs, Interviews, Success: Everything a Graduate Needs to Know* (Management Books 2000, £14.99); *Excel at Interviews* (Lifetime Careers Publishing, £10.99).

Chapter six
Accommodation

This chapter covers:

- University accommodation
- Renting privately
- Choosing who to live with
- Finding a house
- What to look for
- Deposits

- Inventories
- Tips for happy households
- Council Tax
- Bills
- DIY
- Renting in England and Wales
- Renting in Scotland
- Renting in Northern Ireland
- Nowhere to live
- Lifesavers

A comfortable home, where you're happy living, will help you study effectively and make the transition into student life much easier. However, the term 'student housing' is so familiar for a reason – you're not going to be living in the lap of luxury on a student loan. But that shouldn't be an excuse for people to rip you off. Knowing your basic rights and how to spot substandard housing will give you a head start.

The cost of your housing will also be the largest chunk of your budget (see *Making the pennies stretch*, page 81). Check out the costs of university campus, off-campus and private accommodation for universities round the country at www.bunk.com

The students' union and university accommodation office have details about university accommodation and private sector housing available in the area. Many have lists of recommended landlords, landladies, housing associations and agencies. See also the information on deciding where to live in Chapter one and Chapter eleven.

University accommodation

The type and variety of university accommodation differs greatly. There has been a trend in recent years to build 'student villages' where houses and halls are grouped around communal shared facilities like launderettes, bars, cafes and gyms. Generally, you are likely to be offered:

- a single or shared room in a hall of residence

- a room in a shared student house or flat

- a place in a student village complex.

You pay your hall, student flat or house fees to the university. Each university has its own criteria about when fees should be paid, but if you get the option then pay them as soon as you arrive. Once you have met the biggest single expenditure you have, it is easier to see what you have left to live on. See also *Making the pennies stretch,* page 81.

Halls of residence

'Hall of residence' describes a vast spectrum of buildings. You could end up living in a huge concrete tower block or in an old building overlooking a courtyard. Most, however, are purpose-built with single study bedrooms, although some have twin beds so you might end up sharing a room.

'Sharing a room is decidedly not for the ham-handed. My room-mate had a very beautiful suede jacket, which came to grief one night when in my clumsiness I tipped a wax candle down it. Nearly the end of a beautiful friendship.'

Cherry Canovan, graduate, Durham University

A single study bedroom in a hall of residence is pretty much the same everywhere. You'll have a bed, a desk, a chair, some shelves and somewhere to store your clothes. There are obviously variations and additions to this theme, such as a sink and more floorspace, but those are the basics you can expect. Increasingly, you can also expect telephone and internet access in your room. And sometimes even an en suite bathroom or shower room, which is a fantastic bonus. Shared student bathrooms can get pretty grim. Your hall will be full board (where all your meals are provided), part board (where some of your meals are provided) or self-catering.

'I had envisioned horrible people and having to share dirty public loos but in fact it was really good – there are even some rooms with an en suite! It's good to be on campus as everything is right there. But you have rules in halls and there are more distractions because the entertainment is right there.'

Phil Marsh, second-year engineering student,
Warwick University

Halls are run by a warden who usually lives in. Some wardens are postgraduate students. Make friends with your warden or at least always be polite to them. Your warden is the first point of contact in an emergency or if you have any questions or complaints. Some larger halls may have committees of student representatives who help decide on the plans for any development work, decoration, policy and budgets.

There'll be hall rules enforced by the warden. These are designed to make sure particularly antisocial behaviour, such as constant noise, isn't allowed to run riot. For example, you'll usually have to get permission to hold a party. Make sure you know what the rules are.

The obvious advantage of living in hall is that you don't need to worry about bills, cleaning, landlords, plumbing or even, in catered halls, food. Halls are usually near to the university and students' union, which makes it much easier to get involved. However, you may not like the people you're living with or you may not be able to cope with the noise. Don't panic if this happens to you, particularly in the first few weeks. There's inevitably a period of adjustment while people get used to living with each other and away from home. If you're still unhappy later then ask your warden for a transfer to a different hall. You'll usually find wardens and accommodation officers are sympathetic to your problems and do their best to arrange a transfer if a room is available elsewhere.

Food

Fighting over a cooker with ten other people and storing food can be a problem in self-catering halls. And shared kitchen and cooking facilities can become really disgusting after a whole corridor of students has tried to cook their evening meal at the same time. After a few weeks, you may find that the person who has a massive fry-up for breakfast every morning and never washes up afterwards really gets on your nerves. Complain if one individual is responsible for turning the communal kitchen into a pigsty – you'll have the support of your fellow kitchen users. It is more difficult, however, if there are several people to blame. Talk to your warden if the kitchen is becoming a battleground.

Eating hall meals could be a better, if more expensive, option. Breakfast and dinner may be included in your hall fees, but you'll usually have to buy your own lunch. There'll be restricted meal times, which can be a pain if you take part in lots of activities or the dining area is far away from your department or hall. If you're a vegetarian it's particularly important that you make sure there's a vegetarian alternative and the choice is varied.

'The halls here are really nice with a private bathroom! In the first year I was in catered halls, which is a great way of meeting people but more expensive. This year I am cooking for myself, which is perfect now I'm more independent.'

Rhian Jones, fourth-year European studies and French student, Manchester University

Holidays

Many halls expect you to move out and clear your room when term finishes. This isn't a problem if your parents are prepared to act as chauffeurs at the end of each term or you live in halls where secure storage is available. If you have nowhere else to go in the holidays or want to stay in the area then it may be possible to arrange holiday accommodation with the university. Some universities, for instance, run schemes whereby students are given accommodation and spending money in return for office or maintenance work.

Questions to ask about halls.

■ How many places are there and how are they allocated?

- What variety of accommodation is offered?

- How much choice do I have?

- Will I have to share a room?

- Could I stay over any of the vacation periods?

- How many students does the hall house?

- What are the fees?

- Do the hall fees include meals and, if so, which ones?

- What are the catering facilities like?

- What are the rooms like and what furniture do they have?

- Is there telephone and internet access?

- What social/washing/cleaning facilities are offered?

- Is there a bar?

- Is there a sports hall?

- Is there a TV room/common room?

- How many people have to share the bathroom/shower/kitchen facilities?

- How far away is the hall from public transport?

- How frequent is public transport and what's the cost?

- How far is the hall from the university/relevant department?

- Who are the other residents – first-years, third-years, postgraduates?

- Could I store a bike?

- Can I leave things in my room/store things during the vacation?

Student houses and flats

It's quite common for universities to have purpose-built self-catering houses and flats for groups of their students. These can be an excellent way of combining independence with the security of renting from the university.

> 'There is quite a lot of choice, with five different places on campus and some off campus too. We got to choose on a first-come first-served basis. I was lucky because I got my first choice of a student house. I like being on campus and have met people I would not otherwise have met because I'm not just sharing with first-years.'
>
> **Katie Hogan, first-year sociology student,**
> **Essex University**

As in a hall, you'll probably live in your own room, which will have a bed, desk, cupboard and so on, and there'll also be a kitchen, bathroom and maybe a living room, shared by all the residents of the flat or house. The disadvantage is that – as in a hall – you won't get any choice about who you share with. This can be more of a problem in a smaller flat or house than in a larger hall of residence. If you really can't stand your flatmates then go to the accommodation office and request a transfer.

Student villages

Student villages are collections of houses owned by a university and leased to its students. Increasingly, universities are providing this type of accommodation. You may find that the village has been built by a developer, so although it is called university accommodation you may pay your rent directly to the developer or developer's agent. The houses are shared by about seven to ten students, who all have their own room but share a communal kitchen and bathroom.

> 'My accommodation is unusual in that I live in a flat that is described as university accommodation but I pay rent to a different landlord and I don't live on campus. The flats are brand new but some people's weren't ready for when they

arrived at the beginning of term. I didn't have a desk but some others didn't even have a bed!'

Andrew Newsome, first-year maths and computer science student, Nottingham University

Questions about student flats, houses and villages.

- How are people selected to share a flat/house?

- How far away is the university/relevant department?

- How many students live in the flat/house?

- How many people share the kitchens and bathrooms?

- What's in each room?

- Can I stay over the vacation periods?

- What are the fees, when do I have to pay them and who to?

- Is there a warden?

- Who do I contact with any complaints or queries?

- Who's responsible for maintenance?

- Are the residents responsible for keeping the flat/house clean?

- Will I have to bring my own cooking things, cutlery and crockery?

- Is there a washing machine?

- Is there telephone and internet access?

- How far away are the local food shops/markets?

- How far away is the local public transport?

- How frequently does the local transport run?

- How much does transport cost?

- Could I store a bike there?

Other university properties

Many universities operate schemes whereby they rent local properties which they then sublet to students. There are sometimes requirements that you have to fulfil, such as being a second- or final-year student, before you're eligible to rent a house or a flat through the university. Some universities also rent short-lease properties. These are flats and houses which can't be leased for long periods of time because they're about to be pulled down or developed. They'll usually be very cheap but there's a real danger that you'll be evicted with very little notice.

Renting privately

It's unlikely that you can stay in university accommodation throughout your time as a student, so sooner or later you'll have to rent outside, usually from a private landlord or landlady. You can share a house or a flat with other students or friends, live by yourself in a bedsit or live in the same property as your landlord or landlady as a lodger. You may want to live in an area with lots of other students or prefer life outside 'student ghetto land'.

'This is the first year that I am renting and I find it really good. The landlady is lovely and I like the house. I prefer it to halls because you have more space and it feels more like a home, not just a bog-standard room. Go to the accommodation office, if you have one, because they are really helpful.'

Jeremy Carlton, PhD biochemistry student,
Bristol University

Shared houses

You'll probably quickly get used to living in a house that isn't in the best state of repair, usually is a complete tip and is shared by more people than it was originally intended to house. Welcome to a 'student house'. Students can't afford to rent palatial mansions, but be careful that you don't end up renting something which is very substandard as you'll land yourself with a whole load of problems.

Under the law, houses (or flats) shared by many people are called Houses in Multiple Occupation (HMOs) and are required to have:

- a proper water supply and drainage

- a fire escape and other fire precautions

- adequate kitchens and bathrooms for the number of people sharing

- clear staircases, corridors and passages.

If any of these things are missing then the council can prosecute the landlord but may also take action against the tenants! So make sure you check. See *What to look for* on page 119.

Choosing who to live with

Even the best of friendships can crumble under arguments about whose turn it is to do the washing up or who used the last of the milk. A list of agreed house rules can help, but it won't protect you from the pain of realising that your closest friends have some living habits that you can't share. Think about how compatible you all are. Your best friend might have a horrible boyfriend or girlfriend or be fanatically tidy. They might be really messy in the kitchen or hopeless with money. These are all things which won't necessarily make them a bad friend but might well make them difficult to share a house with.

If you reach the end of the first year with ten people you regard as good friends and decide it would be really nice if you all moved in together, then split into two or three households. Living with people can be stressful and you shouldn't put all your eggs into one basket. You'll need somewhere to escape to at times.

You might have to decide whether or not to move in with your boyfriend or girlfriend. You'll need to be very sure of your relationship before you take this step. It's traumatic if you have to move out of your home at any point, but if it's coupled with the emotional distress of a broken relationship then it's vile. On the other hand, living with a partner in a strong relationship can help you both handle the pressures of student life and exams.

'I am sharing with friends I made in halls in my first year. It has worked out really well because we all do different courses which means that you are not seeing the same people during the day and in the evening. I'd get bored if I was sharing with all psychology students.'

**Lindsey Wilson, third-year psychology student,
Edinburgh University**

Finding a house

Start looking for somewhere to live well before term starts. You have enough to do at the beginning of term without worrying about where you're going to live and who you're going to share with. Go to your accommodation office and ask for a list of landlords and landladies who rent to students in the area. They'll give you a list of reputable housing agencies, landlords and landladies. Alternatively, try the classified columns of local newspapers or use word of mouth if you already know people in the area.

'I found my house through a letting agency. Some friends had studied here and told me how to contact them. The agency gave us a list of about four or five houses we went round to look at them and chose one.'

**Sukanta Chowdhury, first-year MBA in finance student,
Luton University**

Try to take over a house from another group of students as you can talk to them about the problems they've had during the year and their relationship with the property owner or agent. Ideally, you should always talk to any previous tenants. Forewarned can definitely be forearmed when it comes to dealing with property owners and building matters.

What to look for

Look at a few properties before renting to see what is available, but be prepared to act quickly when you spot a good one. Always go and see a property before renting it. Women should, if possible, take someone with them for security reasons. If this isn't possible let someone know where you're going and arrange to see the flat during the daytime. See also Chapter eleven.

'My last house was in a real state and very expensive. Landlords and landladies can try to exploit you a bit if you are naive, so make sure you know your legal rights. Also, always get a house with central heating – storage heaters are useless!'

Rob Lucas, third-year critical fine art practice student, Brighton University

---

Security

Look at how secure the property is. Ideally, the front door should have at least two locks on it, a Yale and a deadlock, about 30cm apart. If there's a communal entrance then look at the locks on this as well and find out who has keys to it. The windows should also have locks on them.

Fire escapes

Ask the owner about fire escapes. Some owners aren't good at meeting the legal requirements. Generally, in a two-bedroomed shared house the staircase should be isolated by fitted fire doors to the relevant rooms, including the kitchen, where a fire is most likely to start. In larger houses additional measures may be needed, such as fire extinguishers and outside fire escapes. All houses should also be fitted with smoke detectors and you should check that these are working. If you have any doubts about whether the house you are thinking of renting measures up then check it out. Your local housing department (listed on the internet under the name of the council) can tell you what the minimum fire precautions should be. Don't take any risks.

Neighbours

It might seem like a good idea to live next door to the best pub in the area, but you may not think so after you've been disturbed every night at closing time. Look out for potentially noisy neighbours, residential or commercial. Under the Noise Act, making excessive noise between 11pm and 7am is liable for a warning, followed by a fixed penalty of £100 and then the removal of the equipment which is making the noise. These rules are enforced by the council and apply to you as well as your neighbours.

'My advice is to stick to the basic rules like paying the rent on time, keeping the place tidy and not having too many wild parties. It's all right to have a few parties but having loud parties until 6am every night will annoy the neighbours.'

**Katrina Woods, second-year sociology student,
Ulster University**

Heating

Most students choose flats and houses during the summer months, so remember that a nice bright, sunny day can make a big difference to the way something looks. Check what form of heating the property has, how much it costs and if it's included in your rent. High-ceilinged, big-windowed Victorian houses may look attractive but they are very expensive to heat. If you live in a terraced street or flat flanked by neighbours who aren't students, then they'll probably heat their houses well and you'll benefit.

Try to rent a property where you have control over the heating as you might just want to wear lots of extra sweaters during the winter months rather than have huge bills. Whatever you do, don't heat a property using electric fan heaters as these aren't very effective and are extremely expensive to run.

Gas appliances

In 1992 Clare Watkinson, a student at Aston University, died because of a faulty gas heater. Carbon monoxide poisoning is responsible for the deaths of 30 to 40 people each year. Landlords and landladies are required by law to have all gas appliances checked by a Corgi-registered gas fitter every 12 months and keep records of the inspections and any work done, but some don't. Ask to see the gas safety certificate before you move in, as you can't smell the poisonous carbon monoxide that faulty appliances give out. If the gas appliances haven't been serviced for more than 12 months then ask for this to be done before you agree to move in.

There are, however, some basic warning signals you can look for, such as signs of staining, discoloration or sooting around appliances. If you feel sleepy, sick or dizzy after using a gas appliance stop using it and see your doctor. Get it checked at once. Never block air bricks or window vents as they're essential for the gas appliance to work efficiently. The **Gas Safety Action Line** can give you more information on 0800 300 363.

You could also ask for a carbon monoxide detector to be installed. These cost less than £40 and can be found in large DIY stores or online at www.envirotecproducts.co.uk

Gas is highly combustible. If you suspect a gas leak don't turn on any lights or strike a match. Turn off the supply, open the windows and call the **Transco** 24-hour gas emergency line on 0800 111999 immediately.

Electricity

Don't overload sockets or circuits by using adapters. Electrical points and appliances aren't regulated in the same way gas appliances are, but can be extremely dangerous if they aren't in a good state of repair. Have a look and check that the wiring you can see is properly encased and not frayed. Old-style plugs and sockets may indicate that the house doesn't have modern wiring, so ask. Your landlord or landlady should have the wiring tested every ten years.

Structure

Check for signs of damp and rot. Tide marks on the ceiling, walls or floor or recently decorated patches are good indicators of these problems. Excessive damp can harm your health and slight damp can make people with asthma ill. If you decide to rent a house with signs of damp make sure it's listed on the inventory (see *Inventories*, page 124).

Turn on all the taps and try the loo out. Look at the outside of the property. Some signs of damage aren't always visible, but if there are tiles missing from the roof or water marks around the guttering then it is not likely to be the most structurally sound house. Your landlord or landlady is legally responsible for the structure and plumbing of the house, except in Northern Ireland.

'Check the general condition of the place and try to find out how long ago it was last redecorated. If it has been regularly redecorated then that is a good indication that there has been a high turnover of tenants – and there may be a reason why people don't want to stay for long.'

Lindsey Wilson, third-year psychology student, Edinburgh University

Furniture

Check that the house has enough furniture for everyone who's going to be living there and that it's in OK condition. If the house has more furniture than you think you need then ask the owner to store it for you. Don't try to cram it all into a damp attic as this will ruin the furniture and the damage will be taken out of your deposit. If you look around a house that is occupied, check which furniture will be left behind.

Any furniture provided by landlords or landladies has to meet strict fire regulations. Most new furniture meets the criteria, but always check the labels. Be suspicious of old furniture and ask if you're unsure. For more information contact your local **Trading Standards** department (listed on the internet under the name of the council). A copy of the Government's leaflet *Furniture and Furnishings Fire Safety Regulations* is available by calling 0870 1502 500.

The kitchen

Inspect the fridge and the cooker to check that they work. Look at the space available for preparing food and remember that all your house/flatmates might want to cook at the same time. Check what equipment belongs to the house and what belongs to the occupants. Large kitchens are extremely useful in shared households.

Transport

Look carefully at what's available in the area and imagine travelling back late at night alone. Ask how frequently public transport runs to and from town and university, how much it costs, and how late it runs. If you rely on your own car or bike then look at parking and storage facilities.

Deposits

A deposit, usually one month's rent, is paid before you move in to cover the owner against any damage. You also have to pay a month's rent in advance. So before you get the keys to the door you have to pay two months' rent. Your deposit will be given back to you at the end of your contract, providing the property is in the same condition as it was when you moved in. Make sure you get a written, signed receipt for your deposit and don't lose it during the year. Cover yourself by taking several photocopies, as a month's rent is extremely useful at the end of a year of surviving on a student loan.

If your landlord or landlady refuses to give you back your deposit you should wait seven days after your contract finishes and then write asking for either your money back or a detailed letter stating the reasons why they won't return it to you. If you're not satisfied with the reply then take it to your students' union or your local **Citizens Advice Bureau** (see *Lifesavers,* page 136) for advice.

Inventories

Inventories are complete lists of the contents and quality of everything in the house before you move in. The landlord or landlady will draw this up and then you have to sign it. If the property is already damaged in any way, have the damage included on the list and don't sign it until you're completely happy. The landlord or landlady will measure the state of the house contents against this list at the end of your contract, and if anything's been damaged while you've been living there the cost of repair will be taken out of your deposit.

Tips for happy households

Allocating rooms can be tricky, particularly as most houses have one room which is smaller than the others. And if you all really want the same room things can get quite heated. Try to be as fair as possible. If there are three of you sharing then rotate rooms on a termly basis. If there are more than three of you allocate rooms by drawing straws, picking numbers out of a hat or tossing a coin. If someone has to have a room that is much smaller, try to compensate them by them paying a bit less rent than the rest of you.

'I made friends in the first year when I was in halls so I am living with them and another girl who is a friend of a friend. It's worked out very well. There were a few problems at the beginning about washing dishes and cleaning the house and especially about milk! We talked it over and found a system so there aren't any problems anymore.'

Rhiannon Michael, second-year law and German student, Aberystwyth University

It might seem very anal but working out in advance how you are going to divide the bills and household tasks can save on an awful lot of arguments later. It's probably a good idea to organise monthly 'house' meetings too, so you can revise how things are going and make any changes. These don't necessarily have to be serious occasions unless things aren't going well, you could arrange to have a meal together. It can be difficult to bring things up with friends, but it's much better to speak up than leave things festering. So, if it always seems to be you that cleans the bathroom or remembers to buy the toilet roll then say so.

It's also worth talking about how you are going to share any communal areas and things like TVs. This can be a particular bone of contention if you have different favourite programmes that clash or all want to entertain friends on the same night. Discuss how you are going to take turns fairly in the communal areas and on the shared equipment.

And don't forget to be considerate towards your flatmates. Don't crash around first thing in the morning when everyone else is trying to sleep, or come back with loads of noisy mates late at night when everyone else has 9am lectures to be up for. And if you are lucky enough to pull while you are living in a shared house try to think about how your flatmates feel. Of course you will want to spend every night and day with the new love of your life, but your flatmates might not be so keen on gaining an extra (non-paying) member of the household overnight. If boyfriends and girlfriends staying over is becoming an issue you could try agreeing that they will only stay over on certain nights.

You should also remember to ask your flatmates if you want friends to stay over. It might be fun for you but your flatmates might not appreciate tripping over a stranger in their front room when they are trying to get out the door. Always make arrangements with the rest of the house beforehand and try to minimise the disruption to the household.

Council Tax

Students don't have to pay any Council Tax providing they live exclusively with other students. If one person in the house is not a student then, unfortunately, the students in that house are jointly liable for the Council Tax with the person who is not a student. This is something you might want to consider when choosing who to share with.

Make sure you obtain a Council Tax form from your council office as the assumption is that you're liable unless you tell them otherwise. The sooner you're registered as a student the less likely it is that you'll be hounded by bills and court demands.

Bills

Get the gas and electricity companies to read the meters on the day that you move in. If you don't you could find yourself landed with someone else's debts. All utility companies offer different methods of payment but tend to encourage direct debit, where the money is taken out of your bank account (usually in monthly instalments). The company estimates the amount they need to deduct, based on previous usage. They're obliged by law to tell you what these amounts are before the money is taken out of your account. If you pay by direct debit then get your meters read regularly to check your usage is being charged accurately. In a shared flat then set up an account in the name and address of your house into which everyone pays. Discuss and agree on how you're going to pay for utilities before you all move in.

'I set up direct debit for my bills, which is worth doing as it works out cheaper in the long run than paying by cheque since it makes it simpler for the companies.'

Amanda Warburton, microbiology with medical bioscience graduate, Kent University

---

If you fail to pay your utility bills then the supply will be cut off and you'll be charged for having it reconnected. Once you're identified as a bad payer then the payment options open to you may be limited (see *Making the pennies stretch*, page 81).

Don't panic if you get an unexpectedly high bill. Companies do make mistakes and they can often be sorted out over the phone. If you're not satisfied with the treatment you receive then contact the relevant complaints organisation listed in *Lifesavers*, page 136.

There are a number of companies that supply utilities, particularly in urban areas. Shop around for the company that offers the best gas and electricity deals in your area and change the account if necessary. Log on to www.upyourstreet.co.uk or www.saveonyourbills.co.uk to see how the various suppliers compare.

'I found it very easy to get the utilities sorted out. I found out who operated in my area and rang them up. They ask you what your address is and which services you want and then sort it all out for you.'

Amanda Warburton, microbiology with medical bioscience graduate, Kent University

Electricity

There's no connection charge for electricity unless there are outstanding debts. If the bills are going to be in your name contact the company that supplies your electricity and tell them you've moved in. Do this on the first day of your contract. If you're a first-time customer, you may be asked for a deposit or to pay by direct debit.

You can also pay for electricity by having a meter installed. These are run by electronic keys which you take to your nearest charging point. They are good if you don't want to be bothered with bills but a pain if your nearest recharging point is miles away or only open at certain times. Talk to your landlord if this method of payment appeals to you.

'We just divide the electricity bill up between us at the end of each month and that's it. However, we did have a problem with the gas bill when we first moved in. The previous tenants hadn't paid their bill so our first bill was big – around £100. However, we contacted our letting agents and they paid us the money back so it was quite easy to get sorted.'

Sukanta Chowdhury, first-year MBA in finance student, Luton University

Gas

The gas supply should already be connected when you move in. If it isn't then ring the gas supplier and find out if there are outstanding bills for your address. If there are, then contact your landlord or landlady immediately and get him or her to sort it out.

Faulty gas appliances are extremely dangerous (see *Gas appliances,* page 121). If you smell gas then put out any cigarettes or candles, don't turn on any lights because the switches can cause sparks, get out of the property and contact **Transco** on 0800 111 999, open 24 hours a day.

Water

If you get a bill for the water rates it is likely to be addressed to 'the Occupier'. This might not mean you, although you should check your contract. Pass it on to your landlord or landlady if water rates are included in your rent or pay it immediately if it's your responsibility.

Telephone

Ask which company supplies your line. Contact them on the day that you move in and ask for the bill to be changed to your name. Whichever company you use you'll have to pay a standard charge for line rental and for your calls on top of that. If there's no phone line in the accommodation then you'll have to pay to get one installed. Ask for an itemised bill. This will save arguments when you come to divide up your first three-figure phone bill. To compare prices of phone companies in your area log onto www.phonebills.co.uk

'We write all our calls down on a pad of paper next to the phone and our BT bill is itemised so we pay for the calls we each make. The line rental and VAT we just divide equally between us.'

**Lindsey Wilson, third-year psychology student,
Edinburgh University**

TV and rentals

Many companies offer students special offers, especially at the beginning of the academic year. Shop around to get the best deal, but stick to well-known companies. You may be asked for a deposit or to pay by direct debit and your name will definitely be given to the TV licensing authority. To get a TV licence, go to www.tvlicensing.co.uk You need a TV licence even if you are living in halls of residence and have a TV in your room. If you're renting a television and/or a video or DVD player then do this at the beginning of the year as short-term rentals are more expensive.

DIY

Some basic DIY skills save time and money. However, anything major is usually the responsibility of the landlord or landlady, so contact him or her immediately if the bathroom floods or the tiles start flying off the roof.

Changing a fuse

If the lights in one part of the house refuse to come on, then you've probably got a blown fuse. Most modern fuse boxes simply have a switch you need to turn back on (it will be the one that says *off* rather than *on* when you look at the fuse box).

If you need to replace any fuses then go to the main fuse box and turn off the mains switch before you touch anything. You'll know if you have the right switch because the whole house will be plunged into darkness, so take a torch. Check what amp fuse you need to replace. You may find spare fuses are provided but if you need to buy one try DIY shops and places like Woolworths. Replace the blown fuse with the correct amp fuse cartridge. If changing a fuse doesn't work call an electrician.

Blocked sinks and frozen pipes

Sinks can get blocked quite frequently, especially when several people are all trying to force the remains of their supper down them. A plunger will often release the trapped waste. Place it over the plug hole and pump quickly about ten times. Pull the plunger up again and see if the sink empties. Repeat several times and then give up. If the plunger fails, the pipe could be frozen or may have supper remains trapped in the overflow outlet. Try heating the pipe with a hairdryer if it's frozen or taking it off and removing what you find. However, put a bucket under the U-bend before removing anything or you'll be standing ankle-deep in water before you know it. If this still doesn't work then get help.

Your landlord should really deal with pipe insulation, but if there is a cold spell coming on you can take preventative measures to stop pipes freezing by wrapping the pipes in old rags and fastening them with string. Freezing pipes can be a real problem in some parts of the country.

Find out where the stopcock, which turns the water mains off, is in case of an emergency. There may be more than one and they may affect different rooms. Practise shutting the water off before you have a major flood.

Changing a washer

If you have a leaking tap or one that violently shoots water at you every time you turn it on, then you need a new washer. Turn off the water at the stopcock and unscrew the tap. You will find a rubber circle between the tap and the mounting. Take the washer to your local hardware store or DIY shop and find one which matches it. Put the tap back together again with the new washer.

Renting in England and Wales

'We haven't had too many problems when renting privately but the landlord hasn't always been helpful. Sometimes he's too busy and doesn't come when he's supposed to.'

Sukanta Chowdhury, first-year MBA in finance student, Luton University

Renting in England and Wales is governed by the 1996 Housing Act. Your tenancy agreement will be known as a 'shorthold' tenancy. This gives you the right to live in the property for six months unless you and your landlord or landlady agree that the length of your tenancy should be longer. This can be great for students, as owners who are used to renting to students will often allow you to sign a contract just for the academic year so you don't have the expense of renting over the summer holidays. Once you agree with your landlord the period that your tenancy will run for then it is known as a 'fixed-term'. However, the length of time you are able to stay in the property can also be left open-ended. In shared houses ask for a joint tenancy. Put all the tenants' names on the contract so you're all jointly liable. At the end of the day you should end up with a document known as a joint shorthold fixed-term tenancy (although the 'fixed-term' bit is optional) which states:

- the date on which the tenancy begins

- what the rent is and when it's due

- any rent review arrangements

- the length of any fixed-term agreement.

The landlord can ask you to leave at any point after six months, providing that any fixed-term agreements have been completed. You must have two months' notice in writing if the owner wants you out.

The landlord can only have you evicted for certain reasons listed in the 1996 Housing Act, such as rent arrears, antisocial behaviour or damage to the property. He or she has to apply to the courts. Before you can be evicted the courts have to grant a Possession Order. If you're threatened with eviction then get advice from your local **Citizens Advice Bureau** (see *Lifesavers,* page 136) or students' union.

Landlord's responsibilities

The landlord or landlady is responsible for repairs to the outside of the property and any structural repairs, including heating, hot water and things like baths, sinks and taps. He or she also has to make sure the gas and electrical appliances are safe, that the furniture and furnishings meet the fire regulations and that there are adequate fire precautions.

Your landlord or landlady should also give you 'reasonable' notice if they want to visit the property – this is usually thought to be 24 hours. If they regularly breach this it can count as harassment. It's also illegal for them to discriminate against you, for example, on racial or sexual grounds. If you feel you have suffered in this way then go to your students' union or local **Citizens' Advice Bureau** (see *Lifesavers,* page 136).

'The landlord is quite nice and when we need something he does provide it. I didn't have a proper desk in my room but when I asked for one he got one. The only problem is that he doesn't always give the 24-hours notice that he is supposed to.'

Rhiannon Michael, second-year law and German student, Aberystwyth University

Paying rent

Many property owners will want you to set up a standing order at the bank, which your parents may be asked to guarantee. If this is likely to be a problem then find out about how you'll be required to pay your rent before you sign any contracts. If your landlord or landlady asks for a series of post-dated cheques to cover your rent, offer to pay by standing order instead. It can be difficult to cancel cheques at a later date if things go wrong. Keep your own record of your rent payments just in case there are problems later.

There's no legal stipulation about what rent you should be charged. Always compare the rent you're asked for with rents charged for other properties in the area. If you feel yours is too high then you can appeal to your local **Rent Assessment Committee** within six months of starting to rent. Ring your local council (listed on the internet) for details.

New tenants

Find out who's responsible for getting new tenants. One of your flatmates may want to leave early and you might not like the idea of a complete stranger moving in. Usually, the owner will be happy to let you arrange your cotenants, but check the small print in your agreement.

Renting in Scotland

There are two types of tenancy agreement in Scotland – a short assured tenancy, which must last for at least six months, and an assured tenancy, which lasts for longer. When you agree with the owner how long your rent will last you sign a contract. This covers how and when the rent will be paid, how much rent will be paid, who is responsible for the internal and external maintenance of the property and any restrictions on the use of the property. You must have this drawn up in writing and sign it. It then becomes legally binding.

When your short assured tenancy is coming to an end your landlord or landlady will serve you with a Notice to Quit. It's important you realise that this doesn't mean you have to leave. If you want to stay in the property then you and the property owner can negotiate an assured tenancy under which you'll have different rights. You need to be clear about which type you're signing.

Anyone renting in Scotland, particularly if they aren't familiar with Scottish law, should look at the information at www.betterrentingscotland.com and download the *Student Renting Guide* from http://scotland.shelter.org.uk/advice/advice-1271.cfm Your student advice centre will also be able to help.

'We are having a few problems because the landlord doesn't have the money to carry out the repairs. We can't use the washing machine at the moment. My advice would be to try to get an objective opinion from the previous tenants when the agency is out of earshot.'

Lindsey Wilson, third-year psychology student, Edinburgh University

---

Renting in Northern Ireland

Tenancies in Northern Ireland are governed by the Rent (NI) Order 1978 and generally fall into two categories – controlled tenancies and uncontrolled tenancies. Uncontrolled tenancies give you fewer legal rights and protections. Controlled tenancies can either be restricted or regulated. You should make sure that you are signing a *controlled regulated* tenancy if your rent is more than £1 a week. In Northern Ireland it is not the automatic responsibility of the owner to carry out repairs, so check the terms of your agreement carefully. Some of the deposit you are asked for may also be non-returnable.

Anyone unfamiliar with the law in Northern Ireland should get information and advice from their students' union and download the *Students' Housing Guide* from the **Housing Executive Northern Ireland** at www.nihe.gov.uk

---

'I went through the university student services to find my house. You tell them how many of you want to share and they issue you with a list of houses and flats that have the right number of rooms. Our landlady is really lovely and we haven't had any problems. We contact her when we need something. For example, we didn't have a washing machine and she installed one for us – we have been very lucky.'

**Katrina Woods, second-year sociology student,
Ulster University**

Questions to ask when renting privately.

- Will it be a joint tenancy agreement and how long will it be for?

- How are new tenants chosen?

- How will I have to pay the rent?

- How much is the deposit and can I have a signed receipt?

- Can I see the current Corgi gas certificate?

- Are bills included in the rent?

- Will I have to arrange to have the utilities connected?

- How is the property heated and how much does it cost?

- What condition is the plumbing and wiring in?

- Have there been any major structural repairs in the last 12 months?

- What security provisions are there?

- What is the surrounding area like?

- How far away are the shops/transport/supermarket, etc?

- How frequently and how late does public transport run?

- When can I move in?

Nowhere to live

There may be times when you find yourself without anywhere to live, or you may want to arrange short-term accommodation over the holiday period. Your accommodation office or students' union can supply you with a list of bed and breakfasts and hostels in the area. Hostels can be useful if you find yourself without a roof over your head – some offer short-term lodging of up to 28 days, which should give you plenty of time to sort out some permanent housing.

Bed and breakfasts will place limits on how long you can stay. They can also be very expensive, particularly if you have to eat out. Both bed and breakfasts and hostels should only ever be used as emergency accommodation. Don't try to live by moving from one place to another as this will seriously disrupt your study.

Lifesavers

Start with your *university accommodation office* and *student's union*.

If you need more specialist advice then your local **Citizens Advice Bureau (CAB)** can advise on contracts, your rights and any problems you have with landlords or landladies. You can get advice online or details of your nearest local CAB branch from **National Association of Citizens Advice Bureau** at www.nacab.org.uk

Shelter gives advice to those needing housing and can put you in contact with local housing organisations. Call the emergency housing helpline on freephone 0808 800 4444 or contact the Shelter office closest to you. Details are on the website at www.shelter.org.uk

Chapter seven
Transport and travel

This chapter covers:

- Public transport
- Bikes
- Cars and motorbikes
- University travel schemes
- Getting away from university
- Travelling abroad
- Places to stay
- Working abroad
- Lifesavers

Getting to and from university is not only a necessity but needs to be budgeted for (see *Making the pennies stretch*, page 81). How you travel will depend largely on where you're studying. If you study in a small town then your feet or a bicycle are likely to be the best method of getting you from A to B, whereas if you study in a city then you'll soon become familiar with the public transport networks. Anyone studying in a very rural location may have to consider getting their own set of motorised wheels.

'I go everywhere on foot. I don't live on a campus but I still find it easier to walk. It also doesn't cost anything. I sometimes borrow my friends' bikes as I've never actually got round to buying my own.'

Rob Lucas, third-year critical fine art practice student, Brighton University

Public transport

If you are going to be relying on public transport to get around (and most students do) then look at the savings you can make by buying monthly travel passes. It might look like a lot of money to shell out all at once, but they usually work out much cheaper than buying a ticket every day. And investigate all the discounts you can get. Showing your NUS card (see *Students' unions,* page 33) may in itself give you a reduction. You should also get a Young Person's Railcard (£20, www.youngpersons-railcard.co.uk 08457 48 49 50) which saves about one third on all rail journeys and lasts for a year, and the year-long NX2 Coach Card (£10, www.nationalexpress. com) which also gives a third off most journeys.

There may also be regional student discount travel schemes. For example, students in London can get reduced tube, bus, tram and Dockland Light Railway travel. You need to pick up an application form from your university (if it is registered with the scheme). More details from the **Student Discount Travel Scheme** helpline on 0870 443 1045. While students in Northern Ireland get cheaper bus and train travel through the discounts offered by **Translink** (www. translink.co.uk).

Ask at your students' union office about schemes in your area – if you don't ask you may not get!

'At the beginning I had never travelled alone to London before or used the tube but after I'd done it a couple of times it was OK.'

Vicky Spencer, third-year textile design student, Chelsea College of Art and Design

Bikes

Many students find that a bike is a cheap and effective way of getting around, and most towns now include cycle tracks in their urban developments. The maintenance for a bicycle is usually quite manageable even on a student loan and cycling helps keep you fit too. You'll need to make sure that you have a proper solid D-ring lock for your bike and somewhere safe to store it overnight.

If you haven't got a bike you can pick them up quite cheaply secondhand. Look in local classified ads or ask at a local bike shop – most have a range of second-hand bikes on sale alongside the brand spanking new versions. Second-hand bikes are less likely to be attractive to thieves too.

Cars and motorbikes

Unless you study in a very rural area it probably isn't worth taking a car to university. The tax, insurance (which may be more expensive for your university town than your home area), MOT, servicing and petrol will be a very big chunk of your not very large budget, and you may well find yourself inundated with requests for chauffeur services. If you do ferry friends around you're allowed to accept payment to help cover your costs but you need a licence to taxi people for profit. Without a licence your insurance is invalid.

Motorbikes and scooters can be a better option for rural areas but remember the insurance and maintenance costs.

If you do take your own transport to university then you'll need to make storage and security arrangements before you leave home.

'I use a car. I'm lucky because my parents pay my car insurance and I worked out that the price of petrol is about the same as buying bus tickets all the time unless you get a bus pass. But I find it much more convenient with a car, especially since this year I'm not living on campus. And if I want to drink one evening I can just take the bus.'

**Phil Marsh, second-year engineering student,
Warwick University**

University travel schemes

Some students' unions run their own transport schemes. These vary wildly and can range from a women's minibus service late at night, to deals with local taxi firms for students stranded with no means of getting home. Your students' union will advertise such schemes during freshers' week, so look out for details.

'There is a university hopper bus that can take you between the branch of the campus that's close to my flat and the main campus but it's always really busy.'

Andrew Newsome, first-year maths and computer science student, Nottingham University

Getting away from university

Reducing the number of times that you travel away from university is one of the ways you can save money see *Making the pennies stretch*, page 81. However, going away doesn't always have to break the bank. Check university noticeboards or intranets where you can sometimes find offers of lifts to major cities or events. See if your parents or friends would be able to give you a lift. Invest in a NX2 Coach Card and a Young Person's Railcard (see *Public transport,* page 138). These give about a third off all your journeys and both last for a year. You'll need to take a passport-sized photograph and proof of your age or student status.

Travelling abroad

The years at university are often the only time when people have the freedom to explore far-flung climes. However, it is also the time when this has to be done on a very strict budget. The travel operators have picked up on this and the competition is fierce for student discount fares. Always shop around for the best quote. Visit your nearest student travel shop; some students' unions have one on site or try the internet. Student travel shops are the best source of advice on the various student discounts available.

'I am looking on the internet for cheap flights as I am planning a trip to Madrid with friends at the moment. It's cheaper to fly at certain times of the year so we buy tickets during the cheaper months. There are also travel agents that work with the university to provide cheap tours for students. If you go in a group it is cheaper.'

Sukanta Chowdhury, first-year MBA in finance student, Luton University

Once you know where you are going then pick up a travel guide like *Rough Guides* or *Let's Go Guides,* which cover most countries you are likely to travel to. They have information on what you need to do before you travel and local information for when you're there.

Flights

STA Travel is the largest student travel company and you may find that your campus has a branch on site. If not visit the website for details at www.statravel.co.uk However, all travel companies should offer student discounts on flights and you can get some great last minute deals on the internet, particularly if you can be flexible about when you travel or even where you go.

It's also worth getting an International Student Identity Card (ISIC). An ISIC card (£7) gives you discounts in the UK and thousands of overseas discounts. You also get reduced cost long-distance phone calls, free email and voicemail, commission-free currency exchange and access to the 24-hour emergency ISIC helpline, which you can call from any part of the world by reversing the charges. So if you have a medical, legal or accommodation emergency, help is just a phone call away. All full-time students can apply for an ISIC card and part-time students under 26 can apply for a Youth Travel Card, which gives much of the same discounts. Further details from www.isiccard.com

---

'I went to STA Travel and got flights for Malaysia which weren't exactly cheap but were cheaper than they would have been otherwise. I also use the internet to find cheap flights and when I got my ISIC card they sent me information about how to get discounts.'

Rhian Jones, fourth-year European studies and French student, Manchester University

---

You can also reduce air costs by taking a courier flight. This is where companies pay a significant proportion of your flight in return for the use of some of your luggage space. However, the company using you as a courier sets your arrival and departure times and these may not fit in with your travel plans. You can find details of cheap flights at www.courier.org

Whichever travel company you book through, always check to see if it is a member of the Association of British Travel Agents (ABTA) and if it isn't don't book a flight with it. ABTA acts as a guarantor for all agents registered with it, so if the travel company fails to supply the goods your expenses should be refunded.

Inter Rail

Travelling by train might be a more viable option on your budget. You can get an Inter Rail card, allowing you to travel for a set period of time through 26 countries divided into 'zones' in Europe and the Mediterranean. A one-month, all-zone card costs £285 if you're under 26. You can buy it from any major national rail station, through a student travel agent or online by visiting www.interrailnet.com

Coaches

If you can cope with being in a confined space for a long time then a coach ticket is much cheaper than going by plane or rail. But budget for food as you'll have to pay for your food and accommodation if it isn't a sleeper coach. You can get tickets for the licensed Eurolines company from any National Express agent. There are unlicensed companies that will be cheaper but they might not follow all the safety laws that govern licensed companies. For more information and to book online visit www.nationalexpress.com

Hitchhiking

Hitching can be a great, cost-effective way of travelling around but make sure that you are sensible about your safety (see also Chapter eleven). If you can, always hitchhike in pairs. You should also find out about the laws which govern hitching abroad so you avoid hassles with the local police. Different countries have different hitching codes, so ask what code operates where you are. If you use the thumb signal in some countries you'll actually be giving prospective lifts the equivalent of the V-sign, which isn't the best way to encourage people to pick you up! Check a travel guide for the etiquette that applies to the country you are visiting.

Hitching can be a great way to meet people and get personal tips about the best places to visit in the area. Be prepared to wait for a long time before getting a lift and always have a 'plan b' in case you don't get anyone stopping for you at all. Don't rely on hitching if you have a train, ferry or flight to catch – splash out on public transport.

'I went hitching round Ireland with two friends. We stayed in hostels and before we left in the morning we asked the staff there to write the name of the place we wanted to hitch to that day in Gaelic. So we had bilingual signs and no trouble with people stopping to give us a lift.'

Tracy Beadle, graduate, Aberystwyth University

Places to stay

If you haven't got a string of relatives and friends across the globe – and most people haven't – then you'll probably end up staying in a mixture of different types of accommodation. Below is a selection of the ones that are most likely to be within your budget.

'The best way of staying somewhere cheaply is to sort out the accommodation once you arrive there, which is what we did when we went to Greece this summer. There are always lots of people advertising accommodation at the airport and it's cheaper than sorting it out from over here.'

**Katrina Woods, second-year sociology student,
Ulster University**

Youth hostels

Youth hostels are cheap but vary considerably in the rules they enforce. Some will have a certain time by which you have to be back and will expect you to help out with the chores. You may also be expected to sleep in single-sex dorms. Others are more lenient and allow men and women to share a single room, don't lock the doors at a certain time and allow you to cook your own meals. You should be able to get a discount if you show your ISIC or NUS card.

Find out more about what's available, how you can join the YHA and book hostel places both in the UK and overseas online and by phone: **Youth Hostel Association** Customer Services (within UK) 0870 770 8868; (outside UK) (+44) 1629 592700; Reservations (within UK) 0870 770 6113; (outside UK) (+44) 1629 592708 www.yha.org.uk

In addition, you can book hostels through the **Scottish Youth Hostel Association** at www.syha.org.uk

There are also numerous independent youth hostels not run by the YHA. You can find details at Hostelling International www.hihostels.com or try www.hostels.com and www.hostelworld.com

Pensions

Pensions are cheap hotels and you don't usually have to meet any particular criteria in order to stay there. You can stay in a single or shared room. The facilities vary though, and pensions often don't provide meals, so shop around. They can be very convenient and are often situated in the centre of town.

Hotels

While hotels in the UK may be well over your budget they can be a bargain abroad, so don't dismiss them because you think they'll be out of your league. In Eastern Europe, Asia and Africa in particular, hotels are very cheap when judged by Western European standards.

'I stayed in a fantastic hotel in India. We were waited on and got brilliant service and food – absolute luxury for about £5 a night!'

Pippa Dauking, graduate, University of Hertfordshire

Under the stars

Camping is a good, cheap form of accommodation while travelling. However, remember that some campsites are a fair distance from the town centre, which might be a problem if local public transport isn't good. If you're travelling the countryside, though, this is not a problem and you can end up in some really beautiful areas. Make sure you check the local rules about camping – a local travel guide will give details. Always ask the landowners permission (if not an official site), clear up after yourself and make sure that all fires are well and truly out with no smouldering embers.

Sleeping on beaches or in railway stations is obviously a free option but be careful that you're not robbed during the night. Thieves are very adept at taking your rucksack out from under you while you sleep. If you're Inter Railing, kill two birds with one stone by arranging to travel to your next destination on an overnight train. Again, watch out for your luggage and make sure you wake up in time if your destination is not the last one on the line.

Working abroad

'I used the bits of my student loan that I could save to fund my travelling but I also combined work with travel. I've been to Canada with BUNAC and I found a job in the Rocky Mountains. I went to Slovenia on an exchange programme for science students. I've also been cycling around Iceland and Inter Railing. Travelling doesn't need to be expensive – there are a lot of scholarships and travel funds about.'

Jennifer Hogan, fourth-year natural sciences student, Clare College, Cambridge University

You can afford more comfortable travel and accommodation if you earn money while you're abroad. There are many ways of doing this – from participating in well-established schemes such as those run by **BUNAC** (www.bunac.org.uk) or **Camp America** (www.campamerica. co.uk) to organising your own vacation work. Ask your students' union for details of schemes that your university participates in.

There are also various websites that carry details of vacancies. Try www.seasonworkers.com and www.payaway.co.uk Or get hold of a copy of *Summer Jobs Abroad* (Vacation Work Publications, £10.99) or *Work Your Way Round The World* (Vacation Work Publications, £12.95).

Checklist for travelling abroad.

- A *Rough Guide* or *Let's Go* guide for the country/countries you'll be travelling in.

- A good quality rucksack and penknife – not to be kept in your hand luggage if flying.

- Make sure your passport is valid for the duration of your holiday!

- Check with the relevant embassy to see if you need a visa or by logging on to the Foreign Office's site at www.fco.gov.uk

- Take out adequate travel insurance.

- Make sure you've had all the necessary injections (ask your doctor).

- Take some basic medicines with you, including sun cream and mosquito repellent spray and a toilet roll.

- Check the availability of contraception as you can't always buy condoms over the counter.

- Take a travel alarm clock.

- Carry all money in a money belt under your clothes.

- In some countries it's better to have US dollars, so you may want to take traveller's cheques in dollars and some dollars in cash.

- Don't take too many clothes with you. Just make sure you have something waterproof, something warm and something cool, something to protect you from the sun and a very comfortable pair of boots or shoes.

- Don't pack your rucksack too full as you may want to collect things on the way.

- Don't take anything valuable with you. Leave your jewellery and watch at home.

- If camping, check your tent before you leave – it may be too late to get more tent pegs when you're there. Also take a mallet and roll mats.

- Take a sleeping bag even if you're not camping.

'I like travelling because I feel independent and far away from everything. I am able to control what I do each day. And obviously you are also seeing different cultures and broadening your horizons.'

**Jeremy Carlton, PhD biochemistry student,
Bristol University**

Lifesavers

For details of student discounts, cheaper fares and suggested accommodation for independent travellers visit the STA branch nearest you or visit the website at www.statravel.co.uk

To apply for or update your passport pick up a form from the Post Office which gives the address of your nearest passport office. If you have any questions or if you need a passport urgently, call the **UK Passport Service** advice line on 0870 521 0410 or visit www. passport.gov.uk for details.

For country by country travel advice, safety advice, information about vaccinations and a host of other things you should know before you go abroad, visit the Foreign and Commonwealth Office's website at www.fco.gov.uk

Publications

For comprehensive information on any country that you're thinking of visiting, get hold of the relevant guide to that country such as the *Rough Guides* or *Let's Go* guides. They are written in an easy-to-follow style and contain information about what to do before you travel and when you get there.

You may also find useful *The Backpacker's Handbook* (Higher Education, £11.99) and *The Rules of Backpacking* (The Vanguard Press, £8.99).

Chapter eight
Health and stress

This chapter covers:

- Health services

- Making an appointment

- Alternative therapists

- Medical charges

- Staying healthy

- Women's health

- Men's health

- Special needs

- Common illnesses and health problems

- Serious illnesses

- Emotional problems and mental health

- Eating disorders

- Problems adjusting to student life

- Lifesavers

How are you going to get organised enough to cook for yourself, let alone register with a doctor? Why does the term 'freshers' flu' sound so familiar? How will you make friends? What happens if you get lonely? And what happens if it all gets too much?

'Keep your body clock in check, especially in the first year, when there is a real pressure to stay up late during the week so it can be hard to get up for lectures.'

**Allan Jones, third-year geography student,
Lancaster University**

Health services

Larger universities have dedicated health centres or health services just for the use of the students. You can see the staff at health centres about:

- mental and emotional problems

- sexual health and contraception

- illnesses

- injuries

- drink and drug related problems.

There may also be specialist clinics, such as counselling and physiotherapy services, and a dental practice. The number of staff will vary according to the size of your university, but they will all be very experienced in treating the issues that commonly affect students.

If your university doesn't have a dedicated health centre then it will have a reciprocal arrangement with one or more doctors' surgeries, family planning clinics and dentists in the area. You will be given details or ask at your students' union.

Wherever you register you need your National Health Service (NHS) medical card, even if you have been asked to bring a medical form from your previous doctor. If you've lost your medical card go to a local surgery and fill in an application for a new one.

'I haven't been seriously ill but I have had tonsillitis and stomach aches. I went to the doctor who gave me a prescription. I registered with a doctor a few weeks into the first year and so there was no problem seeing one.'

Rhiannon Michael, second-year law and German student, Aberystwyth University

---

Remember to register with a dentist as well. You may have to try several before you find one that is not oversubscribed. Some hospitals provide emergency dental treatment, but this is not a method you should rely on. (See also *Registering with the health service*, page 28.)

Making an appointment

Most of the time you need to book an appointment over the phone. Some surgeries operate 'drop in' times where you can just turn up and wait but these are getting less common. If you urgently need to see the doctor, tell the receptionist and ask for an emergency appointment. If it is out of hours – there will be an answer machine telling you who you need to contact. In really urgent cases go straight to the nearest hospital accident and emergency (A&E) department.

When to dial 999

Emergency services get tons of hoax calls each year; however, if someone needs urgent medical attention then it is OK to dial 999. Use your judgement but here are some illustrations of when you probably need to call an ambulance. If someone:

- is bleeding heavily

- has a broken bone

- cannot breathe properly

- has been knocked unconscious

- might be having a fit

- is showing signs of serious illness

- collapses, fits or gets extremely paranoid after taking drugs

- is showing signs of poisoning or overdose

- has persistent chest pain for more than 15 minutes.

Alternative therapists

If you're not happy with conventional medicine then talk to your doctor about alternatives. Many doctors have a positive attitude to homeopathic medicine, which uses natural herbs and products to treat ailments. Other practices such as acupuncture and osteopathy are also recognised as beneficial. However, there's always a danger, particularly when you're feeling ill and vulnerable, that you'll be persuaded into believing in some apparently magical cure. Stick to alternatives which already have an established reputation and talk to your doctor.

For information and a list of practising homeopathic doctors, clinics, hospitals and pharmacists, contact: **British Homeopathic Association,** Hahnemann House, 29 Park Street West, Luton LU1 3BE. Tel: 0870 444 3950, www.trusthomeopathy.org

Medical charges

Full-time students under 19 are entitled to free medical treatment. This includes prescription charges and dental treatment. Students under 18 are eligible for free eye tests. Once you pass your 18th or 19th birthday you have to go through the mound of paperwork that proves you are on a low income. Tackle this early, particularly if you need medication on a regular basis, as it can take a month or longer for your claim to be assessed. Pick up the relevant form (*HC1*) and leaflets which explain benefits, refunds and how to claim them – they are available from doctors, dentists, opticians and hospitals or you may find that your students' union has a stock. You can also order it online from www.ppa.nhs.uk Young people living in Wales get free NHS prescriptions and dental treatment up until their 25th birthday.

Staying healthy

Of course, by far the best thing is to try to avoid getting ill in the first place. It's not quite as simple as 'an apple a day keeps the doctor away' but you can do lots of things that will help you stay fit and healthy. Particularly if you are feeling stressed (see *Stress and anxiety,* page 167) it makes a real difference if you stop eating processed food (sweets, chocolates, crisps, ready-made meals, etc), take some regular exercise and make sure that you get enough sleep – try it and see!

See also the information on drink and drugs in Chapter nine.

A healthy weight

There's not much we can do about our general body shape, just as we can't change the colour of our eyes. If you eat healthily (see below) then your body will stabilise at a weight which is healthy and normal for you. The easiest way to work out if you're the correct weight for you is to work out your body mass index (BMI). Take your weight in kilos and divide it by your height in metres squared. A 'normal' range is between 20 and 25. Your BMI shouldn't be below 18 and if it's over 30 then you're overweight, medically speaking. If you need to lose weight seek advice from your doctor.

Healthy eating

It's tempting to skip meals when you are having a busy time and money is tight, but you will quickly get very run down if you don't eat properly. You can eat good, healthy food on a budget. In fact, avoiding buying ready-made, processed foods will save you loads and will be much better for you too.

Your body needs food to survive and you can't fully participate in things if you lack energy because your diet is poor. There are numerous theories about what constitutes a good diet and opinions seem to change every six months. You can't follow the latest fads on a student grant so stick to the general principle that your diet needs to consist of:

■ carbohydrates – bread, pasta, rice, potatoes

■ protein – meat, fish, eggs, pulses

■ fat

■ vitamins

■ fibre.

Eat 'peasant-style' and base your meal around carbohydrates and vegetables. Added protein can be supplied by a little meat, poultry or fish, or if you're vegetarian, eggs, cheese, dried beans and lentils. Fresh fruit provides extra vitamins and fibre. Eat at least two good meals a day, preferably three. Fill yourself up on bread and potatoes rather than chocolate and biscuits. Carbohydrates provide better nutrition, are cheaper and less fattening. Never, ever cut back on food as a way of saving money. It will make you ill, and if your health suffers your social and academic life will suffer too. For ways to shop cheaply, see *Making the pennies stretch*, page 81.

Recipes

You can usually spot who has gone to university by the food they cook. Some 'stock' student recipes are given below. They can combine any variety of ingredients and all cost around £2 per helping.

'My main problem was that I couldn't cook and I'd never had to do my own food shopping before! My friends taught me to cook – we would try out a recipe together and did group shopping.'

Natalie King, first-year management science student, Loughborough University

Cheats' sauces

Here are two very quick and easy sauces, which can be poured over pasta and/or any combination of vegetables, meat or fish.

Fry some vegetables until soft then add a tin of tomatoes, with herbs and seasoning to taste. Heat through until hot but don't boil.

Gently melt a tub of cream cheese in a saucepan or in the microwave. Stir in enough milk to turn it into a sauce-like consistency. For an extra cheesy hit add grated cheddar, or a teaspoon of mustard if you fancy something spicy.

Pasta bake

Alternatively known as pasta 'à la whatever happens to be in the fridge'. Cook the pasta by following the instructions on the packet and add two teaspoons of oil (this will stop the pasta sticking together). Add some cooked vegetables, tuna fish, bacon or whatever you like to the pasta. Put the pasta and vegetables etc into an ovenproof dish and cover with a cheats' sauce. Put into a medium oven (gas mark 4/350°F/180°C) for about 15 minutes until the top goes crispy. You can also use a tin of soup instead of sauce.

Particularly good ingredients for this recipe are sweetcorn, tomatoes, onions, carrots, tuna fish and, if you feel like treating yourself, mushrooms and sweet peppers. It stores well, so you can make a lot and eat it the next day.

Risotto

Another recipe to which you can add any variety of ingredients. A good rule of thumb when cooking rice is that you need 1½ times as much water as rice. Half a cup of rice will feed one person.

Fry your chosen vegetables, meat or fish in a large pan. When they are nearly cooked, add the rice and a tablespoon of tomato purée and fry for about two minutes. Dissolve a stock cube into the amount of water you need to cook the rice (you'll need more than one cube if you're cooking for more than one person) and add the stock to the pan. Bring to the boil, turn down the heat, then cover the pan and leave it to simmer for the length of time your rice packet says the rice needs to be cooked. Check it every now and again to make sure it's not boiling over or sticking. If there is any excess water left after the rice is cooked, take the lid off and boil the water away.

Soup

Choose whatever you fancy – seasonal root vegetables are particularly good and make very cheap soups. Fry, steam or boil your ingredients. Add a pint and a half of water and a couple of stock cubes, salt, pepper and any herbs. Leave to simmer until it reduces in quantity and the solid ingredients soften. Put through a blender or mouli if you have one and like smooth soup. Serve with a chunk of fresh bread. For a special occasion you can add cream to the soup.

Jacket potatoes

Put cleaned, large potatoes in a hot oven (gas mark 7/425°F/250°C), check them after 45 minutes and every 10 minutes after that. You'll know they are cooked when the skins go crispy and you can easily put a fork or a skewer through the potato. Add anything from cheese and baked beans to tuna and mayonnaise.

'Pasta! I eat any food that is easy – so pasta and sauce, tins of beans, things like that. Chicken is also quite cheap and is easy to cook. I look for bargains – if you go to a shop just before it closes, meat is reduced. I don't eat microwave meals because I find they are not worth the money.'

Jonathan Clayton, third-year biochemistry student, UMIST

Health warning

■ Never eat anything past the 'use by' date.

■ Never leave food out, particularly if it is cooked.

■ Never eat anything with mould on it. It is not good enough just to cut the mouldy bits off as mould puts down long roots. Throw it away.

■ Always store raw meat at the bottom of the fridge below cooked food.

■ Always reheat food to 70°C (very hot) in the centre for at least two minutes.

■ Always wash the work surface in between preparing different food stuffs, particularly if you're preparing meat.

■ Always keep the kitchen clean.

■ Always contact the local council's pest control department immediately if you spot any pests.

There are a few student cookbooks on the market so if you are looking for a last-minute gift suggestion for a relative why not suggest that they buy you one from this list. All give cheap, healthy, quick recipes with students in mind (and their frequent lack of cooking and storage facilities).

The Essential Student Cookbook: 400 Foolproof Recipes To Leave Home With (Headline, £6.99); *Nosh 4 Students* (www.nosh4students.com £5.99) and *Student Grub* (Clarion, £1.99).

Getting enough rest

Sleep deprivation is used as a form of torture. If you don't get enough sleep then you will quickly become run down, find it difficult to concentrate and become irritable and clumsy. It's almost inevitable that you will have the odd late night, but try to 'catch up' by having an early night once in a while too.

Different people can need different amounts of sleep. You will know yourself if you are someone who needs your eight hours in order to feel human. Try not to 'make do' with less too often.

If you experience regular sleep problems, such as insomnia, it could be a sign of stress (see *Stress and anxiety,* page 167) or underlying problems. Talk to your doctor.

Keeping fit

There have been many studies which show that students perform better academically after they take aerobic exercise. Some form of exercise also helps you fight off common germs. You don't need to go to extremes – simply walking quickly enough to make you breathe a bit heavily for 20 to 30 minutes, three times a week will help. Try walking up stairs rather than taking the lift and getting off the bus or train a stop earlier.

If you are interested in doing more rigorous exercise then students usually have lots of access to gyms, swimming pools and sports facilities without having to pay expensive membership fees. Grab this opportunity to try out something new or continue with a current interest. (See also *Sports and socs*, page 34.) Exercise is particularly good if you think you might be stressed (see Chapter nine).

Smoking

The best thing you can do to improve your health is to stop smoking. Smoking also burns a hole in your very tight finances. The students interviewed in a MyEquifax/NUS survey (see page 81) ranked ciggies as the number one vice to give up when the pennies were tight, followed by alcohol.

The benefits of not smoking start the moment you put out your last fag. Within a few months your lung capacity increases significantly and after several years your chances of getting cancer return to those of a non-smoker. However, university is often the time when people become addicted to cigarettes, as free from the constraints of living at home their consumption increases. The more you smoke, the more damage you do to your health and the more difficult it is to give up. Even smoking the odd 'social' cigarette is risky and choosing low tar brands doesn't reduce the risk at all.

If you need help to give up talk to your pharmacist about patches, gum and other nicotine replacement therapies. You can also get information and support from **Quitline** on 0800 00 22 00 www.quit.org.uk

Women's health

Many women prefer to be seen by a female doctor. You have the right to choose, so if your practice does not have a woman registered with it then ask for a list of Well Woman clinics or practices with registered women doctors available in the area.

Breast examinations

Examine your breasts once a month, ideally just after your period, as this is when the breasts are smallest and any changes are more visible. Check for any nipple secretions, changes in the nipple, lumps, dimples or swelling. Your doctor, Well Woman clinic or family planning clinic can show you how to examine yourself correctly. If you notice any changes don't panic, as the vast majority are completely harmless, but go to your doctor as soon as you can.

Cervical smears

Cancer of the cervix can usually be cured if it's caught early enough. The tests are slightly uncomfortable but not painful. Every woman should have a smear test once every three to five years. Your doctor will send you a letter when your smear test is due. If you don't get a letter then ask for an appointment. The test only takes a few minutes and is well worth undergoing for the protection of your health.

'I had a smear test because I changed from the cap to the pill. Within a year I had gone from a completely clear test to one which showed pre-cancerous cells. Because it was spotted in time I was declared fit after laser treatment. I don't even want to think about what would have happened if I hadn't followed my doctor's advice to have regular tests.'

Graduate, School of Oriental and African Studies, University of London

---

Toxic shock syndrome (TSS)

Toxic shock syndrome (TSS) is believed to be caused by using tampons. Typical symptoms are quite similar to those of the flu virus, followed by diarrhoea, high temperature, vomiting, skin rashes on hands and feet, double vision and hair loss. These symptoms develop quickly and must be treated immediately as women can die from TSS. Tampon manufacturers recognise the potential dangers of tampon use and most include detailed instructions on how to use them safely. However, always use the correct absorbency and change them regularly.

Men's health

Men should get into the habit of examining their testes every month and checking for any changes or signs of abnormalities. If you find any lumps or changes they're likely to be harmless, but get them checked out by your doctor, not least for your peace of mind. Young men do get testicular cancer, but there is a good chance of treatment and cure if it is caught early enough.

Special needs

If you have any special needs then you should ask your doctor to put you in touch with support groups close to your university. It will be useful to know a group of people who know the area and with whom you can share your experiences. If you have any difficulty tracking support groups down then contact **Skill** (listed in *Money*, page 79).

'If there is a group for people with the same special needs as you then join because you can find out how others cope. You may not think that you have a big difficulty, but if there is support available to you from others you should take it.'

Claire Baldwin, third-year history student, Aberystwyth University

Common illnesses and health problems

There is a great temptation, particularly when you first get to university, to burn the candle at both ends. If you're doing this while trying to get used to living away from home for the first time, then you're likely to encounter the range of maladies known as 'freshers' flu' and come across some common health problems.

To find out more about common illnesses and health problems and how to treat them yourself go to the **NHS Direct** website at www.nhsdirect.nhs.uk and search for the topic you need information about.

Acne

It's very common for young people to suffer from acne. Washing your face twice daily with hot water and a little non-perfumed soap will help. For regular acne, talk to a pharmacist about products such as tea tree oil that should help within about a month. If over-the-counter products don't help, or your acne is severe, then talk to your doctor who can give you prescription remedies or refer you to a dermatologist if necessary. Doctors are very sympathetic about the misery severe acne can cause and there are a range of treatments available.

The Acne Support Group – PO Box 9, Newquay, Cornwall TR9 6WG. Tel: 0870 870 2263. www.m2w3.com/acne/home.html

Flu, colds and coughs

These usually strike when you're run down, and can rapidly do the rounds in halls of residence. There's still no magic cure, but you can do certain things to make yourself feel better. Try taking paracetamol or aspirin, tucking yourself into bed and drinking lots of fluids. See the doctor if your symptoms persist for more than three days or if you feel worse rather than better.

'The only thing that I really forgot was some form of medical kit. Everyone gets ill in the first couple of months at university, and the last thing you want to have to do is to go to the shops for paracetamol when you are suffering from freshers' flu.'

Elizabeth Hardaker, fourth-year biology masters student, University of Bath

---

Food poisoning

Food poisoning can make you really ill with sickness, diarrhoea and fever. Avoid food poisoning in the home by following food safety advice (see *Health warning,* on page 156) and keeping the kitchen clean. Wash tea towels regularly and use different dishcloths to wipe down the surfaces and to do the washing up. Change these regularly as they can harbour millions of germs. When you are sharing a kitchen it is really important to follow basic hygiene and food safety measures, or you risk ending up with a house or hall full of puking people.

Fast food outlets can also be culprits. Kebabs, burgers, seafood and undercooked meat are the worst offenders, although salads can also be dodgy. Cut down on your chances of getting food poisoning by always buying from busy restaurants and outlets. And remember, if something looks undercooked, it probably is. If in doubt – throw it out. 'Wasting' a few pounds is far better than dealing with the consequences of food poisoning.

If you have severe symptoms lasting more than 24 hours, pass blood or are in severe pain then see your doctor.

Glandular fever

Glandular fever is spread in saliva and is sometimes known as the 'kissing' disease. It usually starts with flu-like symptoms, which carry on for more than a week. However, with glandular fever you also get swollen glands, feel completely exhausted and have a very sore throat and difficulties eating. In some people the spleen and liver may also become infected. If a doctor suspects you have glandular fever then they will do a blood test and throat swab to confirm the diagnosis.

Glandular fever tends to last for at least a month after which you will be advised to return to your 'normal' life slowly and gently. Avoid infecting others while you are ill by not sharing cutlery and crockery.

Hay fever

Hay fever affects about one in five students and can make spring and summer times a misery. Avoiding grass, flower and tree pollens is probably not very realistic, but the good news is that there are a number of effective remedies on the market. Try antihistamine pills, nasal sprays and eye drops from your pharmacist. There are also a number of homeopathic remedies available from health shops or homeopathic doctors (see *Alternative therapists,* page 151). For severe symptoms or year-round problems see your doctor as you may have allergic perennial rhinitis, which is an allergy to dust, mites and pets.

Headaches

These are caused by a number of different things – not just hangovers – and will normally go away in a few hours if you take paracetamol or aspirin. However, if you have severe or frequent headaches then go and see your doctor. If you have a constant headache with fever or your neck feels stiff, call your doctor immediately (see *Meningitis*, page 165).

'I've had colds and flu and stuff. The best thing is to go down to the pharmacy and tell them what you have and ask them what they think is best.'

**Paul Blundell, first-year psychology student,
Lincoln University**

Mumps

In recent times there have been outbreaks of mumps in university campuses. Mumps in itself isn't dangerous, but it can have nasty side effects such as meningitis and infertility in boys – though these are both rare. Symptoms include:

- fever

- tiredness

- sore throat

- headache

- swollen glands

- pain when opening your mouth or trying to eat.

Many young people aged between 14 and 22 haven't been vaccinated against mumps, and the NUS advises that students check. See your doctor who can arrange for you to be immunised if necessary. See also www.immunisation.org.uk

If you get mumps there's not much you can do apart from go to bed and drink lots of cold water (not fruit juice as this stimulates the glands which can be painful) and take a painkiller like aspirin or paracetamol.

Young men who get very swollen testicles as a result of mumps should see their doctor for a stronger painkiller or, occasionally, a course of steroids.

Sore throats

These can be very nasty and make you feel lousy. Try gargling with TCP or soluble aspirin as this may ease the pain. If you don't feel like eating much drink plenty of fluids. See your doctor if your throat doesn't get better after a couple of days, if you can't swallow or if you have earache as well.

Sports injuries

Sprains, bad bruising, muscle pain and swollen limbs can all be a part of playing sports. Most minor injuries can be treated by taking painkillers, muscle heat creams and possibly strapping. If your injuries are more severe then see a doctor who may refer you to a physiotherapist or osteopath. About 75% of sports injuries can be avoided by warming up properly first. Do some gentle jogging and stretching. It's also important to cool down by doing the same thing at the end.

Serious illnesses

These are some student illnesses that require medical attention; you should be aware of the symptoms in case you need to call an ambulance for someone.

Asthma

Most people with asthma are used to managing their asthma. However, cold, exercise, eating certain foods and spending time in smoky places might trigger unexpectedly severe attacks. The signs of a severe attack are blueish skin or lips, gasping for breath, confusion and restlessness. Someone having a severe asthma attack needs urgent medical attention, particularly if their inhaler or other regular asthma medicine is not relieving the symptoms. Call 999 and explain what is happening. Ask what you should do to help the person before the ambulance gets there. Stay calm and make sure you don't leave someone having an asthma attack alone.

Meningitis

Despite the high-profile cases that get reported in the press, meningitis is a rare disease. However, it develops quickly and can kill, so any symptoms need to be taken seriously. It can be caused by both viruses and bacteria, but the bacterial form is more dangerous. The bacteria can spread by prolonged intimate contact such as kissing, but also among people who live and work closely together. It is estimated that students are twice as vulnerable to meningitis as others in the 18- to 25-year-old group – particularly those who live in halls of residence. You can gain protection from some forms of meningitis through injections, and the practice nurse at the doctors' surgery can organise this for you if your immunisations aren't up to date.

The best chance of treating meningitis is if it is caught early. Initial symptoms can be confused with other illnesses, such as flu or having a bad hangover, but someone with meningitis deteriorates more rapidly:

- severe headache

- stiff neck

- dislike of bright lights

- fever and/or vomiting

- drowsiness or going in and out of consciousness

- a red 'pimply' rash that doesn't turn white when a glass is pressed against it (although only about 40% of people with meningitis develop the rash).

Bacterial meningitis can also cause septicaemia (blood poisoning). Meningitis with septicaemia is four times as deadly as meningitis without, though not as deadly as septicaemia without the meningitis. Symptoms of septicaemia include:

- the rash

- fever and vomiting but not in all cases

- cold hands and feet

- rapid breathing

- pain in the joints, muscles and stomach, maybe with diarrhoea

- drowsiness or going in and out of consciousness.

These symptoms can occur in any order and not everyone will exhibit all of them, so if there is any doubt at all call for medical assistance.

For more advice on meningitis contact the **Meningitis Trust** at www.meningitis-trust.org or ring their 24-hour helpline on 0845 6000 800.

Emotional problems and mental health

Everyone experiences difficulties in coping with things at some point in their lives, and around one person in four will experience a mental health problem. It is very common for these to occur during times of change in your life, and moving away from home to start university definitely counts as a time of change. So don't be afraid of admitting that you are having difficulties. There are lots of sources of support at universities from course tutors and students' unions to health centres, doctors and specialist counsellors and psychotherapists.

Loneliness

There is an old student adage, which says that you spend your second two terms trying to lose the friends you made in the first few weeks. This is bound to be true of some people because you're surrounded by so many strangers, so don't worry if you feel you have nothing in common with the first people you meet.

'I barely see the people I spent the first week with now, they weren't the kind of friends you settle with. I did meet loads of people though.'

Susanna Craig, first-year politics and parliamentary studies student, Leeds University

---

It's very easy, especially in the first few days, to look around and believe that everyone has known each other for years. This is obviously not the case. All first years are in exactly the same boat and those people who appear to be completely at ease are probably thinking that you look pretty cool too.

If you find it difficult to make friends there are steps you can take to make things easier. Don't run home every weekend, but give yourself a chance to mix with your university peers. Join a university club where you'll meet people with similar interests. If you find it daunting to walk into a crowded place like a bar or dining room on your own then try meeting people in smaller social situations, like the communal kitchen. Don't take your coffee back to your room, but sit in the kitchen with some reading and you'll meet the next person who comes in to make coffee – not a bad icebreaker.

> 'What helped me adjust was joining sports clubs, like canoeing, which I've done since the first year, where I've met lots of great people and really enjoyed myself.'
>
> **William Wilson, fourth-year management student,**
> **Aston University**

There are people who like to be alone and there's absolutely nothing wrong with this. Solitude is only a problem if it makes you unhappy.

Stress and anxiety

Stress can be very high among students. When you first move to university you have to deal with a lot of changes all at once. The symptoms of stress come in different forms, like feeling tired all the time or not being able to sleep, and you're the best person to know if you're suffering. If your symptoms are extreme then you may be suffering from anxiety.

Don't be afraid of talking about your symptoms, they aren't trivial and you're not alone. Exercise can relieve the symptoms, and there are various relaxation techniques that can help too. Most universities run stress reduction and relaxation courses, which are often free so well worth checking out. You can also get advice from your doctor. You should definitely see a doctor if your symptoms are stopping you from getting on with the things that you would normally do and enjoy.

'Don't struggle in silence. If you are having real problems, see your tutor, talk to classmates, and relatives and friends – you never know where practical and emotional help may come from!'

Deborah Hyde, first-year history student, Birkbeck College, University of London

Depression

Depression is a serious illness that can affect anybody. It can be, though not always, triggered by traumatic life events such as the break up of a relationship, bereavement or financial problems. Depression should be taken seriously, and you need to seek professional medical help if you suspect that you are depressed. Just trying to 'snap out of it' or 'cheer yourself up' isn't going to work.

See your doctor if three or more of these symptoms sound familiar. See your doctor immediately if any of the last three apply to you.

- You feel down and uninterested in things.
- You find that you are frequently tearful or cry for apparently no reason.
- You have difficulty motivating yourself to do anything.
- You don't want to mix with people or socialise.
- You have difficulty sleeping.
- You have lost interest in sex.
- You are not interested in eating or overeat for comfort.
- You use alcohol or drugs to try to escape from your feelings of sadness or to 'help you cope'.
- You deliberately hurt yourself.
- You have suicidal thoughts.

Depression is treated by taking antidepressant medication or through counselling and psychotherapy, or by a combination of these. Antidepressants help alter the chemical balance in your brain which changes when you are depressed. You should start to feel the benefits ten days to two weeks after starting a course and will need to be monitored throughout the treatment. Counselling and psychotherapy help you to understand the reasons why you might have become depressed in the first place and can be very effective at helping you avoid depression in the future. Your student welfare service may have resident counsellors and your doctor can help you find an approved psychotherapist.

Self harm

Some people, particularly young people, deliberately hurt themselves. Most commonly this would be by cutting their skin, severely banging their head, causing deep bruises or taking small 'overdoses' of pills, but it can take many different forms. It is often linked with anxiety and depression, and sufferers describe it as a way of getting rid of negative feelings and stress. If you are self-harming then you need to get advice from your doctor who should be able to arrange a course of counselling and other treatments to help you cope more constructively.

Manic depression

Manic depression, or bipolar affective disorder, is a serious illness that can often occur for the first time in people in their early 20s. It will be very scary for the person affected and their family and friends. It is usually first diagnosed when someone experiences their first 'manic' episode, which can include them embarking on unrealistic, ambitious plans, not making sense to those around them and a general feeling that they can do anything. Manic episodes are followed by periods of deep depression.

During the acute stages of the illness, manic depression is usually treated by a spell in hospital, followed by antipsychotic drugs to reduce the symptoms and regular sessions with a psychologist and/or psychological nurse.

Manic Depressive Fellowship – Castle Works, 21 St. George's Road, London SE1 6ES. Tel: 08456 340 540. www.mdf.org.uk

Schizophrenia

Schizophrenia can also first affect young people in their 20s and is characterised by feeling as though you are being controlled by someone else, having hallucinations, hearing voices and thinking that ordinary events mean something extraordinary. The treatment is very similar to that for manic depression.

Rethink – 30 Tabernacle Street, London EC2A 4DD. Tel: 0845 456 0455. www.rethink.org

Eating disorders

Problems with food often have a variety of underlying psychological causes, and the anxieties brought on by starting university can sometimes manifest themselves as eating disorders.

The main types of eating disorder are:

- anorexia nervosa – when people consistently don't eat as much as they need

- bulimia – a cycle of binge eating followed by starvation or other forms of purging such as making yourself sick

- compulsive eating

- binge eating.

In the United States bulimia is so common among young women college students it is known as the 'college girl disease'.

Doctors are very aware of the serious effects of eating disorders and are sympathetic when approached for treatment. It's vital that you seek expert advice if you have problems with food. Eating disorders can kill people. Speak to your doctor or to the **Eating Disorders Association**, which offers information, advice, details of support networks and publications for both women and men worried about their eating or who have eating disorders.

Eating Disorders Association – 103 Prince of Wales Road, Norwich NR1 1DW. Tel: 0845 634 1414. www.edauk.com

Problems adjusting to student life

'The first year is the hardest in some ways because everything is new and unusual. I was quite shy and so I spent most of my time working – unlike most people! In the second year I moved into a house with some friends and I preferred that because it was a lot more homely and I got on well with my housemates.'

Phil Pearce, fifth-year business studies student, Luton University

Everybody's experience of leaving home and starting university is different, but most people have a few problems adjusting. Anyone who claims never to have had a second thought about the whole process is probably lying. The important thing to remember is that you're not alone.

Avoid as many problems as possible by preparing well beforehand (see Chapter one). If you've spent time thinking about what you need to take and checked that your accommodation is habitable and available then you're likely to have a much smoother transition. And if you do encounter problems don't feel embarrassed about admitting them – there is a network of people at university who will deal with your problems in the strictest confidence. Don't just sit and suffer in silence.

'The biggest problem initially was not having someone you know to turn to in a difficult situation – either a personal one or when you have problems with your course. But that is a problem only at the beginning, you soon realise there are lots of people who can help you.'

Jennifer Hogan, fourth-year natural sciences student, Clare College, Cambridge University

What happens if I've made a mistake?

Don't make any hasty decisions, but if you realise that you've done the wrong thing by coming to university then there's no point in staying somewhere where you're unhappy. Talk to a welfare adviser in the students' union or student health services centre. They'll help identify the cause of the problem and offer advice. If, after talking to people and considering their suggestions, you decide that you still want to leave, then make sure you're aware of the financial implications (see also *Changing course*, page 61).

Lifesavers

Your students' union or university welfare office should be the first point of contact if you have any problems settling into student life, as they have experience of dealing with specific student-related issues. The staff in student health centres can advise on health matters. And make sure that you let your personal tutor know about any problems you have with your studies or course.

Many students' unions also run Student Nightline services. They're great at sorting things out, from how to get home if you're stranded in the middle of nowhere, to what you should do because nobody spoke to you tonight. The telephone numbers are posted round the university or you can get details of your nearest branch from **National Nightline** at www.nightline.niss.ac.uk

If you don't want to talk to someone at university then the **Samaritans** run a 24-hour helpline, which provides a listening ear every day of the year. Call them on 08457 90 90 90, email jo@samaritans.org or visit www.samaritans.org.uk

NHS Direct is a helpline and online information service that can advise on all health matters. The helpline is staffed by nurses 24 hours a day, seven days a week. An operator will make a note of your name and number and take brief details and give you a time when a nurse will ring you back. Call **NHS Direct** on 0845 4647 or visit www.nhsdirect.nhs.uk

Chapter nine
Drink and drugs

This chapter covers:

- Drink
- Behaving badly
- Sex
- Staying safe
- Spiked drinks
- Hangovers
- Alcohol poisoning
- Drink problems
- Drugs
- Increased risks
- Bad reactions
- The law
- Drug problems
- Lifesavers

While at university you will definitely come across many opportunities to drink and will probably be exposed to illegal drugs too. Get sussed about the facts so that you are making informed choices about what you do and never, ever be tempted to do anything you don't want to just to 'fit in'.

Drink

Alcohol is widely available in universities in subsidised students' union bars and facilities. The advantage of this is that you can enjoy a tipple without breaking the tightest of student bank accounts; however, it can also lead to temptation to over indulge.

The current recommended maximum weekly allowance of alcohol is around 28 units for men and 21 units for women. This equates to 14 pints of normal-strength beer or lager for men and 10 pints for women. Alternatively, if you drink spirits, men should not drink more than 28 single measures, and women not more than 21. Regularly drinking in excess of this means you're putting a great deal of strain on your liver, brain, heart and nervous system and damaging your health.

> 'I remember going into town at the weekend and seeing new bars everywhere. These bars are primarily aimed at students, offering lots of really cheap drinks, and encourage people to drink and spend more than they should on alcohol.'
>
> **Andy Bridges, third-year music technology and audio system design student, Derby University**

If you are going to hit the bar then there are some things you can do to limit the damage and help you not to feel so bad the following morning.

- Make sure that you eat a meal before you go out so that the alcohol isn't absorbed straight into your stomach lining. If you've not got time for a full meal at least have a glass of milk and some toast.

- Don't gulp your drinks down and rush for a refill. Drinking quickly means that you can get drunk very rapidly and need to be taken home before the evening has got going. Encourage everyone to keep pace with the slowest drinker in the group.

- Don't buy rounds – just buy your own drinks so that you can drink at your own pace and pocket.

- Drink plenty of water. It's best to drink water while drinking alcohol, but if you can't manage that make sure you drink plenty of water before you go to bed. Alcohol dehydrates you and dehydration is one of the reasons you feel so bad after an excessive night.

Behaving badly

Drinking too much can lead to you behaving in ways that you wouldn't normally. Some people become aggressive and confrontational, while others can get very emotional. Some are tempted to do things that are incredibly foolish and dangerous. If you know that you have behaved this way in the past then avoid getting drunk in public places where you may be vulnerable or in danger. If you are with someone who is behaving badly because they are drunk then try to keep them safe and get them back home.

Sex

Having a couple of glasses of wine to help you feel relaxed and comfortable with your partner is fine, but sleeping with someone when you are off your head is very risky. You may well sleep with people you wouldn't touch otherwise (probably for very good reasons) and are much less likely to use a condom. This leaves you at risk of sexual infections and unwanted pregnancies (see Chapter ten). If you do find that you've had unsafe sex when drunk you should make an appointment to be tested for sexually transmitted infections (STIs) (see *STIs*, page 195), and women should make arrangements to take the morning-after pill (see *Contraception failure and unprotected sex*, page 194).

Never 'take advantage' of someone who is drunk. If they really do fancy you then there will be plenty of opportunities to sleep together when you are both more sober and they will thank you for it in the long run (even if they can't see it at the time).

Staying safe

For safety reasons try always to stick together in a group. If you are drunk and alone then you are extremely open to attack and not capable of looking after yourself. Don't be tempted to take that two-mile walk back home on your own (see also Chapter eleven). Call for a taxi. One taxi fare is definitely worth the cost of your safety, even if it means you can't afford to go out for the rest of the term.

If you are all sober enough to safely make your own way home then it's still wise to check that everybody makes it back OK. You could arrange to text when you are safely inside your front door. If someone doesn't text, then call them to find out what has happened.

'I think it's fine to get drunk as long as you are with your friends, and it's always useful to have one person who is sober to look after the others. It shocks me when I see people walking home at night really drunk and staggering towards the road and they're alone! At every function organised in my halls there has been an ambulance called for someone who has had too much to drink.'

Katherine Lawrey, fourth-year Hispanic studies and history, Birmingham University

Spiked drinks

There has been a slight increase in the number of students having their drinks spiked. This is when so-called 'date rape' drugs are added usually to alcoholic drinks although soft drinks and coffee may also be used. The drugs take effect quickly and can lead to drowsiness, unconsciousness and vomiting. Attackers can then rape, rob or attack their victim.

Although these are relatively rare events, there are some sensible precautions you can take.

- Don't accept drinks from strangers, particularly if they are really pushy – genuine people will understand.

- Try to watch your drink being poured and opened.

- Don't leave your drink unattended – if you have to go to the loo ask a trusted friend to hang on to it for you.

- Buy bottled drinks and keep your thumb over the top.

- If your drink tastes funny or there seems to be more in the glass then don't drink it.

- If you start to feel suddenly really drunk, woozy and/or sick then you may have had your drink spiked – tell a trusted friend and, if you are in a pub or club, a member of staff.

If you are with someone and suspect that they have had their drink spiked, call an ambulance and stay with them until it arrives.

Hangovers

It is probably unrealistic to think that most students are going to make it through their time at university without waking up with a hangover. Hangovers are caused by dehydration, toxins left by the alcohol and low blood sugar. Rehydrate yourself and raise your blood sugar level by drinking something that has sugar in it, like a soft drink, fruit juice or tea with sugar. Many people then have their own 'cures' which can help make them feel better, like a brisk walk in fresh air or a soak in the bath. Find what works for you. However, don't be tempted by the 'hair of the dog' remedy and have another drink. You are simply storing up an even bigger hangover and are damaging your body further.

Alcohol poisoning

There may be times when excessive drinking leads to alcohol poisoning. This is very serious and requires hospital treatment. Symptoms include:

- long periods of unconsciousness
- confusion and aggression
- vomiting
- fits
- slow or irregular breathing
- low temperature and very pale skin.

If you suspect someone has alcohol poisoning then don't leave them alone. They shouldn't be allowed just to sleep it off, as they may choke on their vomit or stop breathing. Call an ambulance and stay with them until it arrives. Don't try and deal with someone who is being violent and aggressive on your own – call the police if necessary.

Drink problems

Problem drinking is often thought of as an older person's illness, but university can be the time when you set patterns that can become dangerous in later years. If you regularly drink heavily in your teens and 20s you are likely to be storing up problems for later. Make sure that you establish sensible drinking habits by not drinking more than the Government recommended amounts on a regular basis and having at least two 'alcohol free' days each week.

Know the danger signs to look out for and seek advice if they apply to you:

- a growing tolerance and the need to drink more to feel relaxed
- drinking to override negative feelings
- feeling as though you need a drink in order to do certain tasks
- becoming angry if you can't get a drink
- spending a lot of time thinking about your first drink of the day and starting drinking earlier and earlier
- getting the shakes if you don't have a drink
- drinking in secret or lying about the amount that you drink.

You can get information about sensible drinking, plus advice on what to do if you are worried about your own drinking or that of someone you know from **Drinkline** on 0800 917 8282.

Drugs

University is a time when you are likely to come into contact with drugs, and around 50% of students admit to taking at least one recreational drug. That also means that 50% of students don't try drugs too. As with anything else, the important thing is not to be pressurised into doing anything you don't want to. If you're tempted to experiment, then find out all the facts first so that you know what you are taking, the possible effects and what the law says.

'The student drug scene is nowhere near as big as it is cracked up to be. I have seen students use illegal substances but I'd seen that before I came to university. Amongst friends I don't really react, it's their choice and as long as I don't think they are developing a problem I will leave them to make their own decision. However, as an elected students' union officer if I see anyone on SU premises using an illegal substance it's an entirely different situation.'

Andrew Stephenson, third-year business management student, Royal Holloway College, University of London

Increased risks

There are a number of factors that make taking drugs much more risky to your health and safety. Don't take chances if you:

- are in unfamiliar surroundings and feel uncomfortable
- have had an argument with the people you are with
- are alone or in a club without anyone you know
- have to buy from a stranger
- are offered drugs as an injection
- would be mixing drugs
- would be taking large quantities of drugs in one go.

You should *never* take drugs if you:

- have a history of mental illness or problems
- have a medical condition that makes it extremely dangerous for you to take drugs, such as high blood pressure, a heart condition, lung problems or epilepsy
- would be sharing a needle.

Bad reactions

Bad reactions after taking drugs can include:

- paranoia and anxiety
- extreme distress
- physical pain, such as cramps and headaches
- dizziness
- vomiting
- injuries caused while high
- blackouts
- irregular heartbeat

- seizures (fits)

- overdose.

If you are worried about the way that someone is reacting having taken a drug then take them somewhere quiet. Stay calm and get them to sip water slowly to cool down. If they continue to feel ill or get increasingly paranoid then get help. Clubs and pubs should have a member of staff who is a first aider. If you are really worried about them then call for an ambulance. You should call an ambulance for anyone who has collapsed or is fitting. Don't worry about getting into trouble. The priority is that your friend receives the medical attention that they need, rather than the legal status of the drug they have taken. Tell medical staff as much as you can about what your friend may have taken. Never, ever leave anyone who is ill after taking drugs alone to just sleep off the effects.

The law

Drugs are prohibited under the law, which applies different penalties for supply and possession. Supply doesn't just mean selling drugs for a living, it can include selling small amounts to friends or even giving them away for free – you don't have to be a drug dealer to be prosecuted for supply. Possession means having a small amount of drugs on you or in your home that the police trust are just for your personal use. If you are found with an amount of drugs that the police feel are more than you would use yourself then you can be charged with possession with intent to supply, which carries higher penalties.

Drugs are also divided into three different classes (approximately reflecting the dangers of taking them) with different penalties.

Class A drugs These are the drugs that carry the highest maximum sentences – up to seven years' imprisonment and a fine for possession, and life plus a fine for supply.

Class B drugs Carry maximum penalties of five years' imprisonment for possession, and 14 years' for supply. You can be fined for each offence.

Class C drugs Possession of small amounts for personal use may be allowed, or you may be cautioned and fined. Supply carries penalties of up to five years' imprisonment and a fine.

These are the maximum penalties and are rarely applied to first-time offenders or people caught with small amounts of drugs. However, you should be aware of what the law says before you make the decision to take illegal drugs.

Getting searched or arrested

The police are able to stop and search you on the street. They can only search your outer clothing, although they may take you to a police station for a more intimate search by a same-sex officer. Searches of orifices can only be carried out by a medical doctor after the arresting officer signs a declaration saying that they suspect a class A drug has been concealed.

The police are able to search your home or room with your permission without arresting you. Once they have your permission to enter your home (even on an unrelated matter) they can carry out a drugs search if they have reasonable suspicions. Other than that, they need to arrest you and have a warrant to search your property.

It's best to cooperate with a police search. Resisting could mean you get hurt and arrested. If you are taken to a police station or arrested ask to see a solicitor, and don't discuss anything with the police until one arrives. Try to stay calm and follow the instructions you are given. Remember that anything you say can be used as evidence against you.

Release runs a helpline for anyone who needs legal advice and produces a 'Bust Card' on your rights and how to react if you are arrested see www.release.org.uk or call 0845 4500 215.

Cannabis

Cannabis, also known as dope, grass or hash, is the most commonly used drug on the student scene. It gives users a heightened sense of colour and sound. Like alcohol, it impairs coordination so don't drive or operate machinery after smoking it and be extra careful when crossing roads. It has no specific addictive properties, but people can become psychologically dependent on it for relaxation or enjoyment. While supply still carries the class B penalties, the laws governing possession are currently class C. This basically means that you are likely to be cautioned for possession rather than arrested. However, the law is under review and possession may be increased to class B.

Speed

Amphetamine, commonly known as 'speed', is the most commonly used illegal stimulant. It is usually snorted, rubbed onto the gums or swallowed, although it can also be smoked or even injected. It gives you a heightened sense of energy, but can have some nasty side effects, such as insomnia, loss of appetite, anxiety or paranoia. Some people feel unwell for a long time when they stop taking speed after continuous use. It is a class B drug unless it is prepared for injection, in which case it is a class A.

Ecstasy

Ecstasy, or MDMA, a common drug on the student scene, is usually produced in the form of a white, yellow, pink or brown tablet. It gives users a surge of energy and the effects can last for several hours. However, it can also lead to feelings of extreme paranoia and insomnia, particularly if you take it when you're feeling unsure about yourself, not getting on with the people you are with, or somewhere you're not comfortable.

Ecstasy has not been around long enough for its long-term effects to be known and has caused a small number of deaths. It's impossible to tell what's in an ecstasy tablet – you could be taking ecstasy mixed with anything from heroin to cleaning powders. It is also a class A drug so carries the maximum legal penalties.

Solvents

The highly flammable fumes from solvents, such as glue, gases and aerosol cans, are sniffed on rags or in jars and bags. Users can feel 'drunk' for a while or have hallucinations. You are also likely to get headaches, vomiting, rashes and your heart will race. It's very dangerous and you risk blacking out and choking on your own vomit – around six people die each month in the UK after sniffing glue.

Magic mushrooms

Magic mushrooms grow wild in many parts of the country and, although it's not illegal to pick them and eat them raw, drying them out could result in a criminal charge and is a class A activity. The effects vary according to your surroundings, whether you feel happy and comfortable or not, and how much you take. Inexperienced users may feel very disoriented and confused, and all users may experience 'flashbacks', where the trip is relived afterwards. If you're worried about someone in this state then stay with them and, if the feelings don't pass, call a doctor.

LSD

LSD or 'Acid' is manufactured illegally in minute quantities which are impregnated into small pieces of blotting paper. It is also sometimes sold as tiny tablets or capsules. Some people experience time slowing down or speeding up and distortions of colours or shapes. 'Trips' can be either good or very frightening. You may experience flashbacks to trips weeks or months after taking LSD. It is a class A drug.

Nitrates

Nitrates (which are also known as nitrites) or 'poppers' are yellow coloured liquids sold in bottles. The vapours are inhaled. The 'high' lasts for a few minutes and may be followed by dizziness, headaches and vomiting. Nitrates are highly poisonous if swallowed and can burn your skin. It is not illegal to possess them but supply is an offence.

Cocaine

Cocaine produces feelings of strength and confidence. However, you can quickly build up a tolerance to cocaine and therefore it's very addictive. Regular users may start to feel depressed and ill. If you're tempted, never, ever inject.

Crack

Crack is a derivative of cocaine that is highly addictive. The 'high' only lasts a few minutes and is followed by deep depression. Frequent users may have hallucinations and suicidal feelings.

Heroin

Heroin produces feelings of relaxation and happiness leading to deep drowsiness and unconsciousness. Tolerance builds up quickly, so higher and higher doses are needed. It usually comes in an impure form, making injecting very hazardous and it's extremely difficult to give up.

Drug problems

Regular drug use can lead to you becoming dependent or addicted. If you find that you are needing more and more of a drug to get the same effects, or that you are using it to help you 'cope' with life, then you have got a problem. Some drugs are highly addictive with horrible withdrawal symptoms such as shaking, vomiting, diarrhoea and hallucinations. If you think you might have a problem then get advice from one of the agencies listed in *Lifesavers*, below, or your doctor. The earlier you tackle it the better your chances of being able to stop taking drugs. The longer you continue the more heavily addicted you become. You end up with a very serious problem that stops you getting on with your life and requires medical support to give up. You may also get a criminal record and/or heavy fines along the way.

Lifesavers

There's comprehensive information about drink and drugs together with sources of support available from the following organisations.

Drugscope – enquiry line 0870 774 3682. www.drugscope.org.uk

Release – helpline 0845 4500 215. www.release.org.uk

Talk to Frank – helpline 0800 77 66 00. www.talktofrank.com

The Site – drink and drugs pages. www.thesite.org.uk/drinkanddrugs

Chapter ten
Relationships and sex

This chapter covers:

- Dating
- The chat-up
- The first date
- Staying safe and sexy
- One-night stands
- Breaking up
- Sexuality
- Contraception
- Contraception failure and unprotected sex
- Pregnancy
- Sexually Transmitted Infections
- HIV and AIDS
- Lifesavers

University can be the time when you meet the love of your life. It can also be the time when you expect to meet the love of your life – and don't. It can be the time when you meet lots of people that you fancy and have fun. It can be the time that you realise that the relationship you had before you started university really is the one for you. And if you don't want to date at all then that is also absolutely fine too. The number of sexual partners you have is not a sign of maturity, and you don't need to have a sexual relationship to prove you're an adult.

Dating

Every relationship is different. Each one starts differently and moves (or doesn't) at a different pace. Dating gives you the opportunity to find out about the dynamics between the two of you and whether you really get on and fancy each other. Do you want to form a relationship and what sort of relationship do you want? Or do you want to break up and go your separate ways?

If you find it difficult to meet people then you may find that your university runs some free romance and relationship websites or speed-dating evenings. Or, if you fancy a more subtle approach, then try joining a few clubs and socs (see *Students' unions*, page 33) where you will meet people with similar interests.

The chat-up

The chat-up is probably the most nerve-wracking part. However, the key to chatting someone up successfully is not about being the best looking person in the room. It has much more to do with confidence (or faking confidence).

- Start by wearing something you feel comfortable in and that suits you (ask friends for help).

- Don't drink too much. One or two drinks are fine, but it is really unflattering and unappealing if you feel that someone is only chatting you up because they are off their face.

- When you spot someone you fancy make eye contact with them and smile – try not to leer.

- Go over and introduce yourself.

- Ask them a question that doesn't just require a 'yes' or 'no' answer.

- Try to avoid clichés (do you come here often) or chat-up lines – they rarely work and will usually come back to haunt you.

- Strike up a conversation where you try to find out whether you share any interests or tastes in music, films or food.

- Subtly try to suss out their body language – if you lean on the bar close to them do they lean in or pull away? Generally if people are prepared to let you 'invade' their natural personal space (about a metre for most of us) then it is a good sign that they might fancy you back.

- If it's going well then suggest that you meet for a coffee or something fairly low key initially.

- If they say yes, swap phone numbers and/or emails. Don't 'pester' them by ringing them immediately but make contact the following day just to say hi.

- If they say no, chalk it down to experience, think about where you might have read the signs wrong and keep your eyes peeled for other people who will appreciate you.

If you change your mind about wanting to meet someone for a date then don't just stand your date up. That is really childish behaviour and you'd be disappointed if your 13-year-old little brother or sister did that. You also don't want to spend all your time trying to 'avoid' them – nigh on impossible in most universities anyway. Instead, ring them up and explain that you have had second thoughts. Never blame someone for you having had a change of heart and try to soften the news by telling them it isn't any reflection on them – they might not believe you but at least they will appreciate that you have made an effort not to be a total toerag.

The first date

Don't make any assumptions about what will happen on a first date. It is the time when you should both feel able to find out more about each other and whether you really do like each other. Try to keep the conversation flowing while you are out, and find out more about each other and any shared interests. Flirt and see if your date flirts back. If you are getting the right signals then move in for a kiss and a cuddle, and sort out a time when you can see each other again.

However, there may be times when you read the signals wrong and things don't go to plan. You may find that your date is actually more interested in being friends. Although it can be disappointing, new friends are no bad thing too. And if it all goes pear-shaped then put it down to experience and try to comfort yourself with the thought that there are hundreds of other people you will meet at university.

Staying safe and sexy

If it all goes well then you will need to have a conversation about safe sex – preferably before you are in the throes of a passionate embrace. Sex is, and should be, fun and fulfilling but it doesn't come without responsibilities. Most students don't want to become parents or catch sexually transmitted diseases. You both need to take responsibility for practising safer sex. Be safe, not sorry.

'The student welfare officer did a speech at the beginning of the first year telling us all we needed to know – the different types of contraception available and the facilities there are to get them. They are available through going to the doctor that you are registered with and there are condom machines in all the toilets here.'

**Katrina Woods, second-year sociology student,
Ulster University**

The only way to be completely safe is by not having penetrative sex. This doesn't mean that you can't explore what turns each other on. Massage, masturbation, kissing and stroking are all safe, sexy ways to explore each other's bodies. However, if you're going to have penetrative sex – and most people do while they're at university – then make sure you're both sussed about contraception (see *Contraception,* page 191).

One-night stands

There's nothing wrong with one-night stands – providing that you are both over the age of consent and clear that is what you want. The problems come when one of you has different expectations. If you only want a one-night stand then be responsible and tell your potential partner. If they agree then tell a friend where you are going – particularly if you meet someone in a club. Remember that even if they say yes –initially they have the right to change their mind at any point, and you must respect that. Practise safe sex (see *Contraception* page 191) and if you make it through to the morning after, make sure that you at least speak to each other and say thank you for a nice evening. Don't just do a midnight flit.

Beware of the student bush telegraph. News about people getting off together spreads like wildfire in a student community, which can be embarrassing. You may find yourself answering questions about your one-night stand six months down the line! Weigh up the pros and cons.

If it transpires that your date wants more than a one-night stand and you don't then you will have to be up front. It's really mean to string someone along and won't do your reputation any favours. Be firm but polite and tell them how you feel.

Breaking up

Break ups can either be amicable or absolutely vile – there is rarely any middle ground. It's also very rare (though not unheard of) that the person you first go out with ends up being the person that you spend the rest of your life with, so sooner or later most people are going to go through a break up. Don't string someone along if you aren't committed to the relationship, and don't put up with someone treating you badly.

There are things that you can do to help make breaking up less painful.

- Don't dump someone by text or email.

- Tell them to their face (or at least on the phone if it is a long distance relationship).

- Explain that your feelings have changed.

- Don't be rude and don't slag them off – it's something that has gone wrong between the two of you, not your partner's fault.

- Give your ex time to say how they feel too, however difficult you find it to listen to.

- Be polite and civilised to each other whenever you bump into each other afterwards.

Some people are able to remain friends. Other people are devastated by the break up of their relationship. Don't shut yourself away. Friends will probably be sympathetic (they are likely to have been there too) and willing to cheer you up. Don't feel bad about calling on them (you can always return the favour). Get them to remind you what a great person you really are and how much your ex is losing out on. It's OK to cry and feel miserable but try to make sure that you eat properly. The pain will lessen over time and you do learn things from each of the relationships that you have. When you feel ready, get back on the dating scene again.

Sexuality

Your own sexuality is up to you to define, so don't feel pressurised, either by peers or sexual partners, into doing anything you don't feel comfortable with. Learning what gives you pleasure and how to talk about this with a partner are part of developing your sexuality. You also don't have to be in a rush to define yourself in any particular way. It's fine to take time to experiment.

If you do choose university as the time to come out as gay, lesbian or bisexual you'll find lots of points of support. Your students' union should have a gay, lesbian and bisexual club where you can meet other students who share your sexuality, take part in activities and receive any support you might need. If there's no such club at your university then ask your students' union about setting one up. You can also talk to and get advice, information and counselling 24 hours a day from the **Lesbian and Gay Switchboard** on 020 7837 7324 www.llgs.org.uk

If, however, your experience of coming out at university is not a happy one then seek support immediately. Gay men and lesbian women should not be put in a position where they are made to feel ashamed or are insulted because of their sexuality. If you're a victim of homophobia then talk to the welfare officer, the lesbian, gay and bisexual group or the lesbian and gay officer in your students' union. Don't blame yourself. Most students' unions have set policies to protect their homosexual students so don't be afraid to speak out.

Contraception

If you are in a heterosexual relationship then you need to agree what type of contraception you are going to use to protect against unwanted pregnancy and sexually transmitted infections (STIs). Most contraception clinics recommend that you use condoms together with another method to be 100% effective. Homosexual couples will need to protect against STIs for which condoms offer the best protection.

You can get contraception free from your doctors' practice, family planning clinics or Well Woman clinics in the area.

Condoms

A condom, also known as a sheath, rubber or johnny, is a thin latex (rubber) cover placed on the erect penis. It offers the best protection against STIs and, if used correctly, is about 95% effective in preventing unwanted pregnancy. Condoms have no side effects on your health.

'It's amazing how many people think condoms only last for a few days. It's a condom, not a yoghurt! They last for years but should not be used after the expiry date.'

Phil Mitchell, former welfare officer, Bangor University

Use condoms that have the heart-shaped British Standards kitemark and don't use condoms past their expiry date – although an old condom is better than none. Read the instructions carefully, as unless you use them correctly you may as well not bother.

After sex, tie a knot in the condom, wrap it in tissue and throw it away. But don't flush it down the loo – loos can get blocked, or if the condom does make it out it ends up in the sea, where it bobs around among the fish for ages before breaking down.

The female condom is similar to the male condom but fits into the vagina. It can take a bit of getting used to and probably isn't for first sexual encounters. It provides the same protection against unwanted pregnancies and STIs and has no side effects on your health.

The pill

There are two main types of contraceptive pill. The combined pill contains progesterone and oestrogen, which work together to prevent ovulation. The mini-pill contains only progesterone, which alters the cervical mucus so that the sperm can't get through, and changes the lining of the uterus so it doesn't accept the egg. Most pills are taken for 21 days and then left for seven days, during which time you'll have a period, but you should follow the instructions on the packet carefully.

The varieties of pill differ in strength, and you will need to consult your doctor or family planning clinic so they can sort out which one is likely to suit you best. You must be open with them. Be prepared to experiment until you find one that suits you.

The pill has a good success rate in preventing pregnancy, providing you take it as prescribed. However, there are certain circumstances that reduce its effectiveness, such as an upset stomach or if you're taking antibiotics. Ask what these are when taking contraceptive advice. The pill doesn't protect against STIs or HIV, so should be used with a condom.

Contraceptive patch

The contraceptive patch works in a similar way to the combined pill but is a small beige patch worn on the skin. You need to remember to change it according to the instructions or it won't be effective. Like the combined pill certain things make it less effective, and a small number of women may experience serious side effects. Your doctor will need to take your full medical and family history. It doesn't protect against STIs so should be used in conjunction with a condom.

Implant

A small flexible rod containing the hormone progesterone is implanted somewhere in the body, usually the upper arm, and can remain there for up to three years. Fertility returns immediately it is removed. It is not suitable for all women and doesn't protect against STIs.

Contraceptive injection

There are two types of contraceptive injection, one that lasts for 12 weeks and one for eight weeks. They can be great for women who then don't have to remember to take the pill. However, they are not suitable for all women and a doctor will have to take your full medical and family history. It can also take up to a year or more for your periods to return to normal once you stop having the injections.

The diaphragm or cap

This is a rubber device inserted into the vagina to cover the cervix up to three hours before sex. It needs to be left there for eight hours after sex. Its effectiveness depends on how you use it and it must be used with a spermicide. Also it has to be fitted initially by your doctor or clinic and should be checked regularly with your contraceptive adviser or doctor. It provides limited protection from STIs and HIV.

Intra-uterine device (IUD) or coil

This is a plastic tubing coil coated in metal that's inserted into the uterus by a doctor and prevents the egg from settling in the uterus. The coil can cause damage to the uterus, which may affect future fertility and cause heavy periods. It is not always effective and can cause serious problems if you get pregnant. It's not usually recommended for young women who haven't had children.

Natural rhythm

The basic idea is that you avoid sex during a woman's most fertile time (12 to 16 days before her next period) but this is very difficult to calculate as women's menstrual cycles can alter dramatically. It involves taking your temperature every day and drawing up charts and doing complicated calculations. You also have to have a very regular cycle for this to be at all effective and a committed partner. The risk of pregnancy is high.

Withdrawal

The man withdraws before ejaculation. This is not a form of contraception as men often 'leak' before coming, and each 2ml of spunk contains about 20,000,000 sperm. Don't believe the old myths about not being able to get pregnant unless a man has an orgasm.

'I haven't really needed to get much contraceptive advice because I see my doctor at home, but I know that if I do want to see someone about it there are people at uni. There is a clinic on campus in the medical centre that gives advice.'

Natalie King, first-year management science student, Loughborough University

---

Contraception failure and unprotected sex

Accidents can happen. If you're in this position then you can take the morning-after pill. Its name is misleading as you can take it up to 72 hours after you've had sex. It is available free from doctors, family planning clinics or sexual health clinics or over the counter at chemists for about £25. It contains a large dose of the normal contraceptive pill and may make you feel a bit sick afterwards.

Pregnancy

Signs of pregnancy are missed periods, nausea, vomiting and breast tenderness. If you think you might be pregnant then burying your head in the sand and hoping it isn't true might be appealing, but won't help you to deal with the consequences. You can buy pregnancy-testing kits from the chemist which are very simple and accurate. If you get a positive result then see your doctor to get it confirmed and discuss the options.

You can get information and advice on your options when facing an unwanted pregnancy, including counselling and abortions offered in centres around the country in collaboration with the NHS from the **bpas** at www.bpas.org.uk

If you choose to have an abortion then the earlier it's done, the safer the operation. You can have an abortion through the NHS or a private clinic. The NHS treatment is free, but you may have to wait for up to eight weeks. Private treatment is quicker but you'll have to pay. The date of pregnancy is calculated from the first day of your last period, unless you're particularly irregular. Abortions are usually carried out between seven and 12 weeks from your last period. If you suffer depression following your abortion seek expert advice from your doctor.

If you choose to continue with the pregnancy you'll have many choices to make throughout the pregnancy and birth, and the more information you can gather the better equipped you are to make these decisions. Read books and contact your doctor for advice and support.

Childcare provision in universities varies greatly around the country. Make arrangements with your tutors and lecturers so they can help you organise your timetable to cover all your work. Ask your students' union about where to go to find out about the extra benefits you can claim.

Sexually transmitted infections

Sexually transmitted infections (STIs) are spread between both men and women through vaginal intercourse, anal sex or oral sex. You only have to have sex once with an infected partner to contract an STI, so it's vital that you protect yourself and your partner. You can't tell by looking at someone whether they are infected or not and the risk doesn't diminish the more times you sleep with them. So, if you're going to have penetrative sex, use a condom.

Signs of STIs

You may have an STI if you notice:

- unusually coloured discharge or leakage from your penis

- unusual discharge from your vagina possibly causing irritation

- sores or blisters around the penis, anus or vagina

- a rash or irritation around the penis, anus or vagina

- a burning sensation or pain when you pee

- a need to pee more frequently

- pain when you have sex.

Some STIs cause only temporary discomfort, but others damage your health permanently. The symptoms can take time to develop, so if you think you've been exposed to any kind of risk don't have sex again until you've been checked out by your doctor, family planning clinic or a specialist genito-urinary medicine (GUM) clinic, also known as a sexual health clinic. You can get a list of local clinics from your doctor or online from the **Playing Safely** website at www.playingsafely.co.uk Counselling is also available at these clinics.

Don't be embarrassed if you think you have an STI – it can happen to anyone who's sexually active, particularly if you have unprotected sex. It's estimated that in the UK one person is diagnosed with an STI every 15 seconds. Here are some of the more common STIs and their symptoms.

Cystitis

Cystitis isn't necessarily an STI. It can be caused by friction during sex, but it can also be an allergic reaction. It's extremely common in women and less common in men, where it is more likely to be the result of an STI than an allergy. Cystitis causes pain when you pee, you feel you need to pee more often, and your pee is cloudy or red. Usually, drinking lots of water, and staying away from alcohol and coffee, and getting an over-the-counter remedy from a pharmacist will clear it up in a couple of days. If not, see your doctor for a course of antibiotics.

Thrush

Thrush causes an itchy vaginal discharge and/or a thick, lumpy discharge in women, while the ends of men's penises become red and sore and they may get little white spots. Bacteria are responsible for thrush and you can get thrush of the mouth, vagina or stomach. Again, it is not necessarily caused by sex. You can buy creams and pessaries from a chemist, but if you have thrush for more than a few days, or if it keeps coming back, then see your doctor.

Chlamydia

Bacteria also cause this STI, which produces vaginal discharge or extra moisture in the vagina, a slight leaking of a cloudy fluid from the top of the penis and pain when you pee. It is passed on through vaginal or anal sex. If you don't have this STI treated with antibiotics then it can cause infertility. Make sure your partner(s) are treated too as they could pass it back to you or on to others.

Gonorrhoea

Women rarely experience any symptoms at all but may well be infected if they have had unprotected sex with a man who has gonorrhoea. Men's symptoms will be a burning pain when they pee, a discharge from the penis and irritation and discharge from the anus. Even though a woman may not show any symptoms she will still need to be treated, so men must tell their partners if they are diagnosed.

Genital warts

Genital warts appear around the vagina, penis and anus and are passed on during penetrative sex. They are caused by a virus and can take a few weeks to a year to appear. Your doctor or GUM clinic can give you a cream to treat them, although the virus may remain for a while.

Genital herpes

Genital herpes is also caused by a virus – some people have just one attack while others have recurring attacks. It results in small clear blisters around the penis, vagina or anus, which burst leaving a very sore area. The blisters are extremely infectious so don't have sex. Not even condoms provide total protection against genital herpes when the blisters are out or burst. In between attacks of blisters you may still carry the virus around in your body but are unlikely to be infectious. However, always use a condom to be on the safe side.

Pubic lice (crabs)

These small lice can be spread by close body contact such as sharing bedding or towels and through sex. They can cause irritation but are easily treated by lotions available from chemists.

HIV and AIDS

The HIV virus is spreading faster among heterosexuals than in any other section of society. HIV and AIDS can affect you, whoever you are. Always take precautions.

The HIV virus is transmitted through blood, semen, vaginal fluids and breast milk. For a person to become infected these fluids have to pass directly into the bloodstream in sufficient quantities – the HIV virus does not survive for long outside the body. There is no risk of catching HIV from everyday social activities such as kissing, sharing crockery, cutlery or food, shaking hands, hugging, swimming in public pools, using public loos, sneezing or coughing.

The high risk activities to avoid are:

■ unprotected penetrative intercourse

■ sharing needles to inject drugs

■ anal intercourse, which is very risky because the lining of the rectum is thinner than that of the vagina and can be ruptured more easily

■ unprotected sex with an infected woman during her period, which increases the risk of contracting HIV by a factor of three.

Should I take an AIDS test?

This is a choice only you can make, and if you think there is a possibility that you've contracted the HIV virus then go for counselling before you make the decision. GUM clinics have counsellors who can talk to you. You may want to consider having an AIDS test before you enter a long-term relationship if you and your partner don't want to continue using condoms. However, you have to be sure that neither of you will have unprotected sex outside the relationship. Don't believe anybody who says they have an AIDS test before each new relationship unless they provide proof.

Lifesavers

Brook offers free sexual health advice and information on contraception, available online or in centres round the country where you can also get pregnancy tests and relationship counselling for under 25s. See www.brook.org.uk or call the Sexwise helpline on 0800 28 29 30 (under 19s only).

FPA offers information on contraception and sexual health, and runs separate helplines for England and Wales, Scotland and Northern Ireland. Online information and contact details at www.fpa.org.uk

Playing Safely has information about STIs and lists of GUM clinics round the country at www.playingsafely.co.uk

Chapter eleven
Keeping safe

This chapter covers:

- Being out and about
- Public transport
- Taxis
- Cashpoints
- On campus
- At home
- If you're attacked
- Date rape drug
- Reporting stolen card
- Reporting mobile phone thefts
- Reporting a crime
- Witnessing a crime
- Lifesavers

Students can be seen as a 'soft' target for criminals – some research estimates that up to a third of all students are the victims of crime in any one year, with young men being more likely to be the victims of violent attacks. While these statistics can seem frightening there are many sensible precautions you can take to reduce the risks of you or your property being targeted.

Being out and about

You can be more vulnerable when you are in an area that you are not familiar with. Whenever possible, try to travel around in a group

– there really is safety in numbers. However, even groups of people can get into trouble, so whenever you are out and about make sure you avoid potentially dangerous situations and stay alert to your surroundings. These safety guidelines apply equally to men and women.

■ Don't take short cuts through unlit or unpopulated areas.

■ Don't dawdle along in a world of your own.

■ Don't listen to your MP3 player/ipod.

■ Don't walk close to bushes and hedges.

■ Don't have a regular routine whereby you always walk back at the same time and follow the same route.

■ Don't carry a weapon – it may be used against you.

■ Do stick to well-lit streets.

■ Do be alert and look back occasionally to see if you're being followed.

■ Do walk at a brisk pace and purposefully.

■ Do carry a personal safety alarm and keep it somewhere accessible.

■ Do wear non-restricting clothes and shoes you can run in.

You can also help by not doing things that might attract attention to yourself. Don't wander along looking like you are lost. Even if you are not sure where you are going walk purposefully. If you need to stop to get your bearings try to do so close to a group of other people, such as at a bus stop, rather than out in the open. Don't flash your mobile phone around, and only use it if you really need to. Disguise any laptops or other equipment you may have to carry round with you in nondescript bags which don't give their contents away. And make sure that your purse or wallet is pushed down well inside your bag or pocket and not visible.

You may feel more confident if you take a self-defence course, where you'll be taught to avoid dangerous situations and protect yourself should you be attacked. Ask your students' union if it runs one, or call your local police station for details.

'I have taken up Taikwondo, mainly because I feel that Coventry (the nearest big city) isn't particularly safe so I feel happier having taken it up.'

**Phil Marsh, second-year engineering student,
Warwick University**

Public transport

If you travel by public transport rather than your own two feet there are additional precautions you can take to protect your safety.

- Don't wait at isolated and empty bus stops and stations.

- Don't get into an empty compartment or one with just one other passenger in it, if you have a choice.

- Don't strike up conversations with strangers, or accept any invitations to get off the public transport and for them to walk you home.

- Do sit next to the driver, conductor, or if you're a woman, another woman.

- Do complain to a driver, conductor, guard or other person in authority if you're pestered or made to feel awkward. Some stations and stops have help points you can use to contact a member of staff.

- Do make sure you leave plenty of time to catch the last bus, train or tube, particularly if you have connections to make.

Find out whether your students' union runs its own alternative transport. This will often be much cheaper, and definitely safer, than relying on public transport.

Taxis

If you're stranded somewhere late at night rather than try to make it back on foot or public transport, it's safer to take a taxi provided you use a licensed firm. Your safety is worth the price of a cab fare.

However, you need to take some precautions when booking or getting into a taxi.

- Don't take a ride in an unmarked car claiming to be a taxi.

- Do ask mini-cab drivers for their identification or make a note of the black cab number.

- Do plan well in advance and use a reputable firm.

- Do ask for a woman driver if you're a woman travelling alone late at night.

Some students' unions run schemes in conjunction with local taxi firms, whereby you can hand over your union card if you haven't got the money to get back home. The firm then invoices the union and you pay when you pick up your card. Ask your students' union whether they have such a scheme.

'If I'm out really late after a night of clubbing I get a taxi back home which takes you door to door, so there is no problem. The last bus is at 11:30pm so I take that if it is not too late.'

**William Wilson, fourth-year management student,
Aston University**

Cashpoints

Cashpoints can be particular targets both for muggings and for cashpoint card fraud. Protect yourself as much as possible by:

- never giving your access PIN number to anybody else – even your best friend

- always getting cash out during the day, if possible

- shielding your hand when you type in your PIN number

- using machines inside banks as far as possible

- never using a machine if something seems wrong with it and it doesn't work as it should do.

If you have to get cash out at night then make sure you use a well-lit cashpoint near a shop or one that you can see other people using safely. Cashpoints in garage forecourts can be good for late night withdrawals. Never use a cashpoint where there is someone lurking around. Remove your card and cash quickly and walk purposefully away, ideally into a public place.

If you suspect that anything suspicious has happened to your card report it to the bank as soon as you can. If your card is lost or stolen then you need to report it immediately (see *Reporting stolen cards*, page 207).

On campus

Burglars can target university campuses, particularly halls of residence. Halls of residence have lots of people going in and out of them at all times of day and night and many rooms containing valuables – an attractive combination for the opportunistic thief. Cut down on your hall being a target by:

- not letting anyone in on your way out

- signing guests in properly

- not telling anybody the security codes – even if they claim to live in hall and have just forgotten it (they will thank you if they are genuine and it means their laptop isn't nicked)

- always locking your room door even if you are just popping out to the loo or to make a coffee

- not allowing strangers to 'doss down' in the kitchen

- reporting anything suspicious to the security staff or warden.

At home

We all like to think that our home is our castle and once we close the door we're safe and sound. While this is true most of the time, burglars are cunning and you need to make things as difficult as possible for them.

- Don't hide your keys outside.

- Don't leave doors and windows open – keep them locked.

- Don't let bushes or gardens get overgrown as they provide perfect cover for burglars.

- Don't let strangers in to use the phone – they may be burglars checking for valuables.

- Don't invite strangers in, even if they say they are a friend of one of your flatmates.

- Don't tell people who ring that you're alone.

- Do draw all curtains and blinds.

- Do fit and use a door chain.

- Do keep some lights on.

- Do make sure there is adequate lighting outside the house which illuminates all potential hiding places, like alleyways or corners.

- Do lock your bedroom door if possible but have the key handy in case you need to get out quickly.

- Do ask to see identification of any 'officials' who call.

Never enter the house if you notice something unusual – the intruder may still be inside. Call the police immediately. They'd rather have a false alarm than have you risk putting yourself in danger. If your house is broken into or the lock tampered with in any way then get the locks changed immediately.

If you're attacked

If you're attacked for your possessions or money the best thing is to give the mugger what they want. Your things are precious to you, but they are not worth getting injured over. You will need to report the crime and cancel your cards and mobile phone (see page 208). You can help reduce the financial impact of being mugged by making sure that your possessions are properly insured (see *Insurance,* page

18). If you need support with the emotional effects of an attack the organisations listed in *Lifesavers*, page 209 can help.

If you are physically attacked, shout as loudly as you can. Don't scream, as some attackers get a kick out of hearing a victim scream, but shout something specific like 'No!' or 'Call the police!' Activate your personal alarm if you have one. If you think you're being followed, go to the nearest lit public place or house and ask to use the phone. Only fight back if you can't escape. If you do have to fight back then poking your fingers in your attacker's eyes is effective and unexpected. Stamping on someone's foot or kicking them in the shins will surprise them and may loosen their grip.

'If I am alone I walk in well-lit areas, but usually I walk with other people at night. I never walk alone late at night.'

Rhiannon Michael, second-year law and German student, Aberystwyth University

Report any attack as soon as you are able to the police (see *Reporting a crime,* page 208).

Date rape drug

There have been a few cases of students having what is termed the 'date rape drug' slipped into their drinks. To avoid this happening to you, don't let strangers buy you a drink and don't leave your drink unattended, which could allow someone to drug it (see also *Spiked drinks*, page 176).

If you suspect that you have been the victim of a drug rape then report it immediately to the police, where a specially trained officer will see you. You can also get support, counselling and legal advice from: **Against Rape,** Tel: 020 7482 2496, www.womenagainstrape.net

Reporting stolen cards

Keep a record of all the numbers you need to report your cards lost or stolen. This only takes a few minutes, and saves an awful lot of panic and additional heartache in the aftermath of any burglary. Gather all the cards you have together, including your bank cards and any credit cards and store cards. You'll need one bill for each card. On the back of it will be the number that you need to ring in the event of you having your card stolen or losing it. Write all of these numbers in one list and keep it somewhere away from where you keep your cards – so not in your purse or bag.

If your cards are lost or stolen then report it as soon as you notice. Most companies won't hold you responsible for any spending that has gone on your cards that you aren't responsible for, providing that you can demonstrate that you contacted them as soon as you realised that there was a problem.

Reporting mobile phone thefts

Help your mobile to be traced if it is stolen by knowing its IMEI number. This is your phone's unique number and you can find it by putting *#06# (star, hash, zero, six, hash) into the keypad. Write this down somewhere safe. If your phone is stolen this number can track your phone and block the thief running up calls at your expense. Call your phone service provider's emergency number (listed on the bills) or the police. If you can't find your service provider's number then ring the Immobilise Mobile Phone Crime Line on 08701 123 123 and they can put you through to the right one.

Reporting a crime

You need to report any crime or violent attack to the police. If you discover a burglary after the thieves have left, it is still important that you report it to the police as you will need a crime number in order to be able to make an insurance claim. In these incidences you should ring your local police station rather than calling 999.

However, if the burglary is recent or you are attacked you should call 999 immediately. The police stand a much better chance of catching the perpetrators if they can get to the scene quickly. Depending on the nature of any attack, you may find that the police officer who deals with your case has been specially trained and can tell you about sources of support available.

When reporting a crime the police officer(s) will ask you a number of questions to establish the facts. You may well be shaken and upset by the event. Take your time and stick to the facts. If you can't remember something or don't know then just say so – there will usually be opportunities for you to add more details as and when you remember them. If you are particularly upset or need medical treatment then the police will arrange a time to take a statement from you later.

You should also report any crimes or attacks to the university authorities too, even if they didn't occur on university property.

Witnessing a crime

If you witness a crime or attack think twice about jumping to someone's aid. There's a risk that you might be injured too and no-one will be able to raise the alarm. Call 999, explain clearly what you are witnessing and wait for the police to get there. They will need to talk to you too.

Don't just walk away from something that looks suspicious. It's true that the police do get lots of hoax calls each year, but if you genuinely feel that you are witnessing a crime or someone in trouble then they would much rather you picked up the phone and let them investigate. It's the prank calls the police want to stop not the ones from concerned citizens.

Lifesavers

For more information about protecting your home and personal-safety courses, contact your local crime reduction officer at the local police station. Your local police station number is listed on the internet.

You can get information about personal safety at home and abroad, including publications and personal safety alarms from: **Suzy Lamplugh Trust** – PO Box 17818, London SW14 8WW. Tel: 020 8876 0305. www.suzylamplugh.org.

If you are the victim of a crime or attack then you can get free confidential information and support from Victim Support. Trained volunteers support people affected by all types of crime and can help with things like going to court. There are regional offices for England and Wales, Northern Ireland and Scotland. Contact details available from **Victim Support** at www.victimsupport.org.uk

Chapter twelve
Life after university

This chapter covers:

- Graduation
- Getting a job
- Being your own boss
- Postgraduate study
- Studying abroad
- Travelling
- Gap Year
- Lifesavers

As your time at university comes to an end, you will have all sorts of choices to make about what to do next. It's a really good idea to spend some time thinking about what you might like to do before you are in the middle of your finals or attending your graduation ceremony. The last UNITE Student Living poll found that the majority of students planned to get a job and start earning as soon as they graduated with 13% planning to travel and 5% planning to go on holiday.

Graduation

Graduation is the time when you get to dress up in your university robes, go up in front of the other graduates to collect your degree, and have your photo taken with proud relatives and relieved friends. It usually takes place a month or two after you have got your results. It's not compulsory – you will get a letter from your university inviting you to attend. Most people say 'yes'. For relatives, in particular, it can be very important to mark this major achievement of yours – even if to you, finals and results seem aeons ago.

Getting a job

Careers advisers recommend that you start job hunting at least six months before you are due to graduate. Employers are aware that competition is fierce and expect to see applications from soon-to-be graduates from this time.

If you are following a course such as medicine, veterinary medicine or law your career can be clearly defined and your course tutors will be able to let you know what the next steps are. For others, though, the decision may not be so clear cut.

'I know I will use my degree in my career. Chinese is a very specialised subject, so I want to use it. At the moment I think I would like to go and live in the East for a few years then come back and do a Masters and generally continue studying to get as many qualifications as possible.'

Samantha Northey, third-year Chinese student, Edinburgh University

---

If you are having difficulties deciding what you want to do then ask yourself some basic questions.

- Would you prefer to work as part of a team or on your own?

- Do you want a job that is office-based or to work outdoors?

- Would you mind putting in long hours or would you prefer to do something that you have more control over?

- Would you like a job that involves dealing with people?

- Would you like a job that involves travel?

- Do you want to do something where you can progress up the management ladder?

- Do you want to do something creative?

- Do you want a job where you can gain professional qualifications?

- Do you want to work for one company or would you like to work on many different projects as a freelance?

Then make a list of the things that you really enjoy and those skills that you think you have. You don't have to restrict these just to what you have learned during your degree or the jobs that you've had. Your hobbies and interests may provide some useful clues too. Enlist the help of your family and friends. They may see strengths (or weaknesses) which you didn't realise you had.

Armed with this information, go to your university careers service. An adviser there can talk to you about your options and maybe suggest things that you hadn't thought of.

'My last job used a lot of what I learned in my degree, but in the job I have now I am using what I learned at A level. I know a lot of people who are doing jobs that aren't related to their degrees at all, but I prefer it this way because I don't feel out on a limb – I will at least know the theory even if I don't know the practice.'

Amanda Warburton, microbiology with medical bioscience graduate, Kent University

---

Vacancies

Once you have narrowed down the types of jobs and areas you are interested in, then you can start your search. Here are the main sources of job adverts, some of which will also be helpful if you are looking for term-time or holiday work.

Graduate recruitment fairs

These are golden opportunities to find out about the sorts of companies that want your services. Companies looking to recruit graduates have stalls where company representatives answer your questions and tell you about the opportunities. Often these representatives will have joined the company the year before as graduate trainees. Make sure you take several copies of your CV so you can leave it with those companies that you are interested in. Take away any literature and make a follow-up phone call to those you are interested in pursuing to enquire about the next steps.

There is a large graduate fair held in London each autumn and some universities also hold their own so ask for details at your students' union or careers service or contact Prospects (listed in *Lifesavers*, page 221).

'I went to my university careers service and they gave me a booklet full of details about which companies would be doing presentations. Presentations are very useful because there are representatives from lots of different companies that you can go and talk to.'

**Samantha Northey, third-year Chinese student,
Edinburgh University**

Job finder websites

Increasingly, jobs are advertised on the internet. There are hundreds of internet sites offering current vacancies, and you can try to narrow down the ones specialising in the field you want to work in by doing an internet search. Or try some of the sites specifically for graduates, which also often have details of term-time and holiday vacancies. Here are some suggestions to get you going.

Get that job – information, advice and vacancies for disabled students at www.skill.org.uk/info/getthatjob/getthatjob.asp

Graduate Jobs – personalised job vacancies sent by email to subscribers, a jobs database and the option to create your CV online at www.graduate-jobs.com

Gradunet – extensive jobs database, job noticeboards and careers advice at www.gradunet.co.uk

Justjobs4students – graduate jobs, plus holiday, vacation and term-time vacancies at www.justjobs4students.co.uk

Milkround Online – a jobs database, career and application advice and updates on employment news at www.milkround.co.uk

Top Graduates – a jobs database, details of graduate recruitment programmes, careers advice and online CV and application forms at www.topgrads.co.uk

Graduate vacancy bulletins

There are two main graduate vacancy bulletins. *Prospects Today*, published weekly from April to September, carries current vacancies and *Prospects for the Finalist*, published four or five times a year, carries details of openings for students when they graduate. Look in your university library, university careers service or have vacancies emailed to you from Prospects (see *Lifesavers*, page 221).

Newspapers

Most local and national newspapers carry job adverts in addition to having weekly careers supplements. Some national newspapers, famously *The Guardian*, carry job adverts that relate to particular fields on specific days of the week, so you need to find out when the jobs you want are advertised. There are also 'job finder' papers, predominantly for local areas. Visit your newsagent to get an idea of what's around.

Trade papers and magazines

Some of the best jobs are only advertised in trade papers and magazines, as employers want to encourage applications from people who can demonstrate an interest in the area by keeping up with industry news. There are some trade publications, such as *The Stage*, which are the only published way of finding out about upcoming jobs in that field. If you are unsure about which publications you should be reading, ask the university careers service, do an internet search and visit a large newsagent. Most trade papers are readily available from large newsagents but a few are only available on subscription, which you can usually use the internet to sign up for. Serious job hunters should subscribe to a trade paper anyway – you'd kick yourself if you missed a golden opportunity because the local newsagent had sold out of magazines the week the job was advertised.

Jobcentre Plus

You might feel that you went to university to avoid Jobcentre Plus, but actually they are really good sources of general careers advice and carry loads of different vacancies, which the staff will also help you apply for. You don't have to be registered with Jobcentre Plus to ask for advice and browse the vacancies, and if you do end up signing on while job hunting then make sure you make full use of their services while you are there.

Connexions/careers services

Connexions/careers services may also be able to help (although Connexions services in England are aimed at 13- to 19-year-olds). They may hold information about some of the fast-track management schemes companies run for graduates.

Recruitment agencies

These can be good, particularly if you want to try out a number of different companies. Many of the vacancies are administrative or secretarial roles for which you may have to be able to type at a certain speed. However, the areas that use recruitment agencies are increasing and now include sectors like IT, catering, teaching, etc. Doing a temporary job can be a good way of getting your foot in the door of a company where you can then make yourself indispensable. If you have languages then specialist agencies that recruit for translators and interpreters can be a great way of finding a job.

Hidden jobs

Over half of vacancies aren't advertised but spread by word of mouth. This means that it is worth sending your CV off to companies, asking if they have any vacancies. You'll need to do your research thoroughly and make sure that you address it to an appropriate named person (either the head of personnel or HR or the head of the department you are interested in).

It also means that it is worth trying to arrange work experience (see *Work placements,* page 94) to try to get a foot in the door. If money is an issue then try balancing work experience with weekend or evening work, but don't do this for too long or you'll end up exhausted and in no fit state to impress future employers.

'I spent some time doing voluntary work for non-governmental organisations (NGOs). It is crucial to have some kind of experience to get a job in the NGO/development field, but it is also really helpful for discovering what kind of work you enjoy doing and where you want to go next. And when a job came up at the organisation I was volunteering at I was offered it.'

Amy North, MSc development studies student, London School of Economics, University of London

Get family, friends and acquaintances to keep their eyes open for you. Many job vacancies are advertised internally on company noticeboards or intranet boards. Call them occasionally or email them so they don't forget to look, as this can be an excellent way of finding out about jobs. It also means that you have a connection with the company that you can mention at interview.

Being your own boss

If you don't fancy the idea of working for someone else then you could work for yourself or set up your own company. It might sound blissful, but this option is definitely not for the faint hearted. To get anything up and running takes a good idea, good selling skills, a lot of hard graft and some accurate financial planning – and that's all before you've been able to draw your first pay cheque. If this idea appeals and you think you've got what it takes then do your research properly and get some advice.

The **National Federation of Enterprise Agencies** helps small businesses get started. Call 01234 354055 or visit www.nfea.com and www.smallbusinessadvice.org.uk

Low cost advice and the help of a personal business advisor is available from **Business Link** on 0845 600 9 006 or www.businesslink.gov.uk.

Young people can get help from www.princes-trust.org.uk and www. shell-livewire.org

If you are self-employed or set up your own business you are responsible for paying your own tax and National Insurance. You can get more details from **HM Revenue and Customs** site at www. hmrc.gov.uk/students

Postgraduate study

'I'd spent so many years learning all about science that I decided I actually wanted to apply what I had learned and do science. Any research post requires you to have done postgraduate education. I'd definitely recommend it. It's very different from a degree – more like a job. It's intense but not stressful.'

**Jeremy Carlton, PhD biochemistry student,
Bristol University**

A growing number of graduates are electing to continue studying. This can be a great way of improving your career prospects and postgraduates usually earn more in their first job than graduates with first degrees. However, postgraduate study costs and you may have difficulty securing enough funding to balance your further study and existing student debt. However, if you get the balance right then it should be very rewarding. You get to study an area that you are really interested in, often with academics who are renowned in their field.

There is a range of postgraduate courses available.

- Doctorates – a PhD or DPhil takes between three and four years after which time you are a 'Dr'. You can also study for an MPhil, which is a shorter course, and you aren't a 'Dr' at the end.

- Masters degrees – in a range of science, arts and business subjects, usually last between one and two years, or can be studied over a longer time on a part-time basis.

- Postgraduate diplomas – usually last about nine months and lead to vocational or conversion qualifications.

- PGCE – the Postgraduate Certificate of Education, for those planning on becoming teachers.

If you are interested in postgraduate study then speak to your personal tutor or get help finding a course from Prospects (see *Lifesavers,* page 221). If you are planning to do a researched-based (as opposed to a taught) course then you need to apply one or two years before you graduate. With taught courses you tend to be able to apply at any time.

Most postgraduate courses (apart from PGCEs) don't come with any automatic entitlement to funding. You need to talk to the university where you hope to study about possible sources of funding. And try the **NUS Funding Finder** at www.nusonline.co.uk Some students combine part-time postgraduate study with part-time work to make ends meet.

Studying abroad

There are opportunities to carry out postgraduate study abroad. This can be great if there is a country or overseas university with a particularly good reputation for your subject. It can also give you the opportunity to broaden your horizons and learn another language fluently. Most British students are entitled to live and work in Commonwealth countries, mainland Europe, the USA, Canada, Japan and many others. The application process might be rigorous and can involve having to sit aptitude tests, submit a postgraduate research plan, undergo medicals and produce a host of supporting residency and education documents.

University careers services are good places to start. You will also most certainly need help from a careers adviser to track down sources of funding. Talk to your tutors too. You may find that they have international contacts who can help.

Travelling

'In my final year of my first degree I decided that I wanted to go back to South America when I graduated, where I had spent my gap year. I had to start planning this a while in advance. I needed to set up and/or find projects to work on and get enough funding to go. Often universities have grants for travel or work abroad, but the application deadlines can be quite early.'

**Amy North, MSc development studies student,
London School of Economics, University of London**

If you are tempted by the idea of putting off joining the rat race and can afford to travel then this could be a good time to do it. It can be difficult to travel once you start working, although some people successfully combine travel with short-term contract jobs or temping jobs.

There are things that you can do while you are travelling to boost your CV and develop skills. Someone who has worked abroad will definitely stand out from the crowd. Depending on where you travel and your experience there will be opportunities to do voluntary work or you can sort out a job in advance of travelling. The organisations listed in *Lifesavers*, page 221, have more information about finding jobs abroad.

'I have decided that I am not going to look for my ideal job when I leave university. I want to travel so I am going to get a job for a year to save money. I don't know what job I'll go for – whatever is available, so that I can save. I still don't have a clue about what job I ultimately want to do.'

**Allan Jones, third-year geography student,
Lancaster University**

Gap year

Not just for 18-year-olds before they start university – gap years are becoming increasingly popular with graduates too. They provide an opportunity to gain some experience, think about what career you would like and broaden your horizons. The opportunities for graduate gap years are now huge and there's a great range of both voluntary and paid work opportunities as well as the more traditional Teaching English as a Foreign Language (TEFL).

However, it can take some time to organise, especially if you have to undergo any training, apply for visas and have medicals and courses of injections. It may also take a little while to put the funding in place. Fortunately, there are lots of organisations that can help to organise gap years and the main players are listed in publications such as *A Year Off… A Year On?* (Lifetime Careers Wiltshire, £10.99), or *Taking a Gap Year* (Vacation Work, £11.95). Be very careful that you know what you are signing up for though when using an organisation, as some of them require you to fund your own trip.

Lifesavers

Your university careers service should be your first port of call for careers advice, help with CV writing and job applications and details of suitable vacancies. The careers/Connexions service local to where you live may also be able to provide information. Look on the internet.

Graduatelife provides information and advice on life after university including choosing a career, getting a job, travelling abroad and buying a house at www.graduatelife.com

Prospects provides careers advice, a graduate forum, a careers planning service and details of postgraduate courses. You can send your CV or application form by email to a careers adviser and they will send their comments back. Prospects also has databases of jobs, both for graduates and for students looking for term-time and holiday work, a database of work experience vacancies and details of careers fairs around the country www.prospects.ac.uk

TotalJobs has a large number of vacancies and provides careers and CV advice, as well as a jobs email service at www.totaljobs.com

Publications

There is a range of publications that have advice on working in a particular area such as publishing, television or management. These tell you more about the industry and provide tips on ways of getting in. Look in large book shops for the area in which you are interested and ask the staff if you can't track down a book on your preferred profession.

There are also many general advice books. Here's a selection to give you an idea of what's available. *The Graduate Career Book: Making the Right Start for a Bright Future* (Financial Times Prentice Hall, £18.99); *How to Win as a Final Year Student: Essays, Exams and Employment* (Open University Press, £14.99) and *Successful Interviews Everytime* (How To Books, £9.99).

What's what and who's who

Campus: The area where the university teaching buildings are. Many also have student accommodation on site and are completely self-contained centres of student life.

Chancellor: Usually a nominal 'head' of the university, brought out on ceremonial occasions to shake hands and pass on congratulations. To make things more confusing this person is sometimes known as a Visitor.

Dean of students: The person, if one exists in your university, who is responsible for your welfare both academic and personal.

Department: The part of your university responsible for teaching your course. You can be part of more than one department if you are studying a joint course.

Director of studies: Also known as the head of department, which is much more self-explanatory. Basically the person responsible for running the department who may also do some teaching as well.

Executive officers: Elected students there to help sabbaticals with anything from making posters to representing students' views to the university.

Faculty: The umbrella grouping of related subjects so that the arts faculty carries out administration for the humanities subjects and the science faculty, the science subjects.

Freshers: The term used to describe all first-year students. You'll get really cheesed off with being called a fresher two terms into your first year by 'mature' second-year students. Ignore them – 12 months from now you'll be doing the same to next year's intake.

Freshers' fairs: Events where the local banks, businesses and students' union clubs and societies all try to persuade you that they are the best thing since sliced bread.

General Union Meetings: These come under a variety of titles, but are basically where all students of the university decide which policies the students' union should adopt and elect the students who are going to run it.

Halls: Halls of residence are buildings where students (usually first-years) live.

Lecturer: A member of the department who gives lectures. He or she probably has a specialist field and researches it when not teaching.

Local Education Authority (LEA): The organisation you have to apply to, for assessment of the financial support you are entitled to (i.e. in England, student loans and maintenance grant). In Northern Ireland this department is called the **Education and Library Board (ELB)** and in Scotland it is the **Student Awards Agency for Scotland (SAAS)**. You need to apply each year or you may end up being asked to pay all your tuition fees.

The National Union of Students (NUS): The national representative body for students. If your college is a member (and most are) then you will get an NUS card, which will entitle you to certain discounts.

Personal tutor: The tutor in your department who's been assigned to look after your welfare. He or she may not be the tutor who teaches you.

Rag: Where students do silly things and have a lot of fun all in the name of charity. Also can be the derogatory, or perhaps affectionate, name for the student newspaper.

The registry: The place where you go to register as a student.

Sabbatical officers: Students or finalists elected by the students of the university to take responsibility for running parts of the students' union. They are paid a salary and are very well versed in student issues having had recent experience of being a student at your university.

Seminars: Group discussions with a lecturer where you have to take your courage in both hands and present a paper.

Student loans: The money you can borrow from the Student Loans Company to support your living costs and tuition fees. Part of your student maintanence loan is means-tested on yours and your family's income and you have to pay it back with interest when you graduate.

Students' unions: Also known as guilds of students, student associations and junior common rooms. The places that provide cheap beer, entertainments, clubs, societies, stationery, food and can help you with any problem in complete confidence.

Tuition fees: In 2006 tuition fees will increase to up to £3000 per year, but you will be able to take out a student loan to pay them which has to be paid back when you graduate. Scottish students studying at Scottish universities don't have to pay tuition fees.

Tutor: The person who teaches you individually or with a small group of other people in a tutorial or seminar.

Vice-chancellor (VC): If you have a VC then he or she will be the big boss who does all the hard work and is responsible for running the university. It gets confusing because these people are also known as principals, directors and deans – it depends on what basis your university was set up on.

Vice-principal: Deputy to the VC.

Welfare adviser: The member of staff (or team) who is responsible for the welfare of all the students at the university. Very helpful, totally unshockable people who have seen it all before. The first point of contact for any difficulties you have while at university.

Index

More titles in the Student Helpbook series ...

helping students of all ages make the right choices about their careers and education.

Jobs and Careers after A levels and equivalent advanced qualifications

Opportunities for students leaving school or college at 18, including advice on jobhunting, application and interviews.

£10.99   ISBN: 1 902876 93 8

New edition
Careers with an Arts or Humanities Degree

Published in association with UCAS

Compulsory reading for anyone considering arts or humanities at degree level.

£10.99   ISBN: 1 904979 06 8

New edition
Careers with a Science Degree

Published in association with UCAS

An excellent read for anyone considering science at degree level.

£10.99   ISBN: 1 904979 07 6

A Year Off ... A Year On?

Published in association with UCAS

All the information and advice you need on how to make the most of your time out between courses or jobs.

£10.99   ISBN: 1 902876 86 5

CVs and Applications

For anyone who is applying for a job or college place; includes how to use the internet in marketing yourself.

£10.99   ISBN: 1 902876 81 4

Excel at Interviews

This highly successful book makes invaluable reading for students and jobhunters.

£10.99   ISBN: 1 902876 82 2

Visit us online to view our full range of resources at:
www.lifetime-publishing.co.uk